"How to" guide

ORGANISING SPECIAL EVENTS

for fundraising and campaigning

John F Gray
Stephen Elsden

6

DIRECTORY OF

CAF

Published by
The Directory of Social Change
24 Stephenson Way
London NW1 2DP
Tel: 020 7209 5151, fax: 020 7209 5049
e-mail: info@dsc.org.uk
from whom further copies and a full publications list are available

The Directory of Social Change is a Registered Charity no. 800517

First published 2000
Copyright © Directory of Social Change 2000
The moral right of the authors has been asserted in accordance with the
Copyright, Designs and Patents Act 1988.

ISBN 1 900360 56 X

British Library Cataloguing in Publication Data
A catalogue record for this book is available from the British Library

Cover design by Lenn Darroux
Designed by Sarah Nicholson
Typeset, printed and bound by Stephen Austin, Hertford

Other Directory of Social Change departments in London:
Courses and Conferences tel: 020 7209 4949
Charity Centre tel: 020 7209 1015
Research tel: 020 7209 4422
Finance and Administration tel: 020 7209 0902

Directory of Social Change Northern Office:
Federation House, Hope Street, Liverpool L1 9E
Courses and Conferences tel: 0151 708 0117
Research tel: 0151 708 0136

Contents

Foreword

Almost since its inception, the Virgin Group of companies has been noted for its special events, be they to launch a new product or service to the media and public, or to breathe new life into one of our existing activities.

At the same time, I have seen the incredible growth in the use of special events by charities and other fundraising organisations. Some of these I have helped to organise, and I have experienced both the struggles that must be overcome and the elation that is inevitable at the end of a successful event.

I have also been privileged to attend many more charitable special events – not only to help raise funds but also to experience their unique entertainment value. For me, the best charitable events enable people to have a good time and raise money into the bargain.

Some of the most memorable events I have attended were organised by the British Red Cross. I am therefore delighted that the authors of this book have agreed to share their experiences, and those of other successful charities, for the benefit of those planning this most exhausting and exhilarating of fundraising activities.

I am pleased to offer up this foreword to the book because I know that within its pages are the innovative ideas and tips that can enable all of us to organise successful special events. My own copy will be close by me in my office.

Sir Richard Branson

Virgin Management Ltd

Acknowledgements

The authors would like to thank the following for their time, support and contributions to this book:

Jeffrey Archer, Jenny Edwards, Uta Hope, Mike Lancaster, Stephen Lee, Ben McKnight, Andrew Napier, Ade Oyneyi, Lyndall Stein, Russell Thompson, Sue Wilkinson, Alexandra Williams

and the following for their inspiration, creativity, advice and support over many years of organising special events:

Geraldine Allen, Simon Cooper, Harvey Goldsmith, Nigel Havers, John Hooper, Nerys Hughes, John Morgan, Clare Rayner, Angela Rippon, Sarah Rodgers, Maria Shammas, David Simons, Neville Shulman, George Smith, Jonathan Stone and the late George Thomas, the Viscount Tonypandy.

About the authors

John F Gray has worked in the voluntary sector for 30 years, and in that period has been involved in producing, directing and organising events for fundraising, campaigning and profile raising. He has performed and produced at venues as varied as the Royal Albert Hall and the local chapel of his home town in Wales. Since 1991 he has worked for the British Red Cross, where he masterminded the 125th Birthday celebrations, championed the British Red Cross Landmine Campaign and worked with volunteer committees in planning and preparation for many significant public occasions.

John is a founder and now a Fellow of the Institute of Charity Fundraising Managers, a Fellow of the Institute of Public Relations, a Fellow of the Royal Society of Arts and a Member of the Marketing Society of Great Britain. He has lectured overseas and in the UK on special events.

Stephen Elsden has been writing about the voluntary sector for over ten years. He helped to found *Professional Fundraising Magazine* in May 1990, and went on to serve as its Editor between 1992 and 1994. He has worked for the British Red Cross since 1995. He has also written articles on fundraising for the *Daily Telegraph*.

Stephen is a Full Member of the Institute of Charity Fundraising Managers and Chair of its Editorial Board.

Introduction

Why use special events?

Special events have never been more popular with charities and other fundraising organisations. They are exciting and motivating for staff, involving and challenging for volunteers, and appealing and rewarding for supporters. They are also, of course, extremely lucrative in terms of the amount of money they raise and the opportunities for publicity and increased public awareness that they provide. But why should that be?

In the mid-1980s, a professor of psychology at Oxford University began an experiment. His aim was to discover what made people happy, and his conclusions were startling for everyone, not least fundraisers. According to the professor's subjects, dancing made them happiest, followed by giving support to a charity. Combine the two and it is easy to understand the popularity of special events in the not-for-profit sector.

In my experience that somewhat clinical experiment is borne out in the real world. When special charity events work, they do so because everybody is having a good time, and in those circumstances people are generally well disposed towards donating money or listening to key messages about charitable work. The act of giving, or simply of listening, enhances their experience at the event.

Conversely, when special events do not work – and most charities will have a few flops at some point in their history – they fail because people are not having a good time. Or worse still, people are so put off by the nature of the event that they do not even turn up in the first place.

The aim of this book is to explore the many facets that make up a successful special event for fundraising or campaigning. While successful events are fun on the day, they disguise the months of planning and determined effort that are essential in delivering that success.

Of course, small-scale events have been a staple of fundraising for decades, and while many of the rules for a local event organiser hold true for those running special events, large-scale occasions have their own unique elements that attract the public and can make them work so well.

This book explores the importance of all those elements. However, it does not pretend to be a textbook on how to actually run special events on the night. There are as many different types of special event as there are ideas in a fundraiser's mind, so such an exercise would be futile. Instead, we take you through the essential tasks in the weeks, months, and occasionally years leading up to the event. Having said that, towards the end of the book, two chapters look at two of the more popular ideas for special events – charity auctions and anniversaries.

As fundraisers, we forget at our peril that one of the greatest of those unique elements is the audience. People enjoy meeting other people – socialising is satisfying and rewarding – and for many individuals the attraction of a special event is to be 'seen' with celebrities, successful business people and local dignitaries. In special events, as in so many other aspects of fundraising, success attracts success.

Although this book is written primarily for special event organisers, I hope that other readers, perhaps those who help out on event committees or those who regularly attend events, will find here valuable information and greater insight into what makes special events work.

It is not the intention of this book to claim that organising special events is easy. However, I hope it will show that with careful planning, and consideration of all the essential elements, many of the difficulties that lay in wait can be overcome, and your own special events should have a greater chance of being the success we all crave.

John F Gray

August 1999

1

Setting your objectives

Tempting though it is to rush ahead and start planning, no truly successful event has ever worked without an underlying strategy and clear objectives for what it should achieve.

This chapter will look at the following topics:
▶ Linking to your strategy
▶ Primary and secondary objectives
▶ Securing senior support
▶ Testing your assumptions

Linking to your strategy

Take a look at your organisation's strategic plan, if you have one. Now, consider what key outputs in that plan might be supported by a special event. It could be that you plan to launch a new service or expand existing services into new areas. An event could help you to promote the development of your services to a wide audience, embracing potential users, likely funders, and even individuals who might take paid or voluntary positions to deliver the service.

Alternatively, your charity may be planning a campaign to promote a health awareness message, a repositioning of your organisational objectives, or even a new name for itself. When the Spastics Society changed its name to Scope several years ago, it did so with the help of a series of media activities, special events and receptions. This helped to promote the new name to many different audiences and did so several times to reinforce the change in people's minds. Scope is now a top household-name charity.

If your organisation does not have a strategic plan, then your director and trustees must themselves have an idea as to where your charity is heading, perhaps expressed in the form of a mission or vision statement. This direction is likely to be explained in your annual report, communications with donors, and maybe an internal newsletter. Every organisation has a sense of its strategic objectives, be they for one year or five. Part of the job of a truly creative fundraiser or PR professional is to suggest the benefits which special events could bring to those strategic objectives.

Events have moved on a long way since the ubiquitous 'High Society' charity balls of the early Eighties. Special events today can have a dynamic and stimulating impact on your charitable objectives, not least because they have the potential to reach so many more people than do traditional activities.

Primary and secondary objectives

Having determined what aspects of the charity's strategic plan your event, or events, will support, you must next decide on the objectives that you hope to meet. This book is called *Organising special events for fundraising and campaigning* as those are the two most common objectives for charity special events – generating income and raising awareness of a particular message or area of work. But there are many other possible objectives, such as recruiting new volunteers for your organisation or re-invigorating existing staff, volunteers and donors to support your cause into the future.

When setting objectives for special events – and, indeed, for any activity – there are two areas in which organisations often go wrong. The first of these is in setting too many objectives, because for any special event to be successful everyone involved in the organisation needs to understand its purpose.

There needs to be a single, clear objective which has to be met and which will help you to make decisions about the various questions – which venue to use, who to invite, what media to promote the event through – that will come up as your planning and organisation progresses. If you have two, three or even more different and potentially conflicting objectives, you will not be able to make those decisions, and your fellow staff and volunteers will be similarly confused in their work. The result will be an unfulfilling experience for everybody and an event that fails to fully achieve any of its objectives.

If your event does need to have more than one objective, you should prioritise them so that everyone is clear which is the primary objective and which are the secondary ones. Never switch these around or your event will again be in danger of losing its direction and your staff and volunteers their sense of purpose. It is also important to keep in mind that the primary objective is paramount – if it is not met, you may find that no amount of success in meeting secondary objectives will alleviate the sense of disappointment felt by those most closely involved.

The other mistake often made with the objectives for special events is that they fail to specify tangible results. For example, who is your target audience for the event? Is it enough to get anybody to attend, or are you trying to attract business people or young people? If you want to recruit new volunteers, how many do you need, and what will they do? If you are marketing your services to new audiences, what level of service do you want to achieve in these new markets? And if fundraising, how much income are you aiming for? The answers to these questions may need to come from other colleagues, but you must know the answers yourself to prevent the event from becoming isolated from the wider goals of your organisation. These results are also essential if you are to tangibly measure the success of your event once it is over.

Fundraising targets in particular should never be overlooked. Money is an inescapable element of all special events, and we will explore budgeting issues in *Chapter 3*. But regardless of your carefully considered income and expenditure streams, if the original target you set is unrealistic, your event is bound to fail before it has begun.

Too many charity directors set wildly optimistic targets for their events, then complain when the results fall short. Do not allow yourself to be pushed into agreeing an unachievable income target. Wait until you have budgeted your event, and then you can say with some degree of confidence how much your event will raise, if all goes to plan.

Securing senior support

As has already been noted, the decisions of your senior directors and trustees can have a dramatic effect on the success of your special event. This is why it is essential to get their backing at the very start of your planning process, so that everyone understands and supports the objectives you are hoping to achieve.

There are two particular benefits to be had from securing senior support. First, if things go wrong and the event does not perform as expected, or even loses money, responsibility is shared at the highest level. The more senior figures who understand the potential risks to your charity if the event fails, the better should be the scrutiny that is applied to your event plan before it is given the go-ahead. What is more, if your directors and trustees all think your event will work, the chances are that it will.

The other major benefit of senior support is the agreement of financial backing for your event. In *Chapter 3* we will illustrate the importance of a break-even budget – that is, at the very least ensuring your event will recover its costs – but any event will need some initial financial investment to get it started. You may need to hire additional staff, travel around the country to find a suitable venue, or produce some marketing materials to help attract sponsors. Any of these will cost money, and you are likely to need support from your director or trustees before you can begin incurring costs while preparing your event.

The best way to get senior figures on your side is to present them with a carefully reasoned business case. This will clearly outline the objectives you wish to achieve, how you expect to achieve them through your event, how the charity will benefit and what it will all cost. The most successful business cases are a combination of firm, tangible information, such as your proposed budget and expected audience, along with more emotional, passionate thoughts on what the event can do for your cause. A suggested structure for an event business case is given in the box.

Structure for event business case
- objective(s)
- anticipated benefits to the charity
- content of event
- budget
- project plan with timetable
- roles and responsibilities
- monitoring and evaluation system
- internal communication and ownership

Testing your assumptions

However strong your business case may be, and regardless of the enthusiasm of your directors and trustees, only one thing will prove if your idea can work: actually running the event. But very few event organisers get everything right first time, so it is worth building a test period into your event plan.

This may entail running a scaled-down version of the event, enabling you to clearly analyse what works and what does not. Alternatively, if you have two or three options for your event and are not sure which one would work best, you could run several concurrent small-scale events, each testing out a different option. Many large organisations will insist on the testing of new initiatives before they will commit funding to a higher profile event.

Even if you decide to go straight ahead and organise the full-scale event, pay special attention to the key decisions you make, and note down their outcomes. If you choose to repeat the event as a national activity from a regional pilot, or run the special event on an annual basis, these notes will be invaluable to your forward planning. When running an event, nothing will give you more confidence than being properly prepared for the issues and problems that may arise.

Checklist for setting your objectives:

- Analyse your charity's strategic plan.
- Set a clear objective for the event.
- If necessary, set a fixed primary objective and several secondary objectives.
- Agree achievable results and targets.
- Use a business case to get senior support from directors and trustees.
- Test assumptions on a small-scale.

2

Encouraging innovation

The proliferation of events, from concerts and shows to sponsored activities and balls, has never been greater and neither has the number of different charities organising them. Yet the number of people who might be attracted to these events has not increased so dramatically in recent years. So, how do you select an event that will be innovative enough to both stand out from the crowd and attract the right audience?

This chapter will cover the following topics:
▶ Evaluating the competition
▶ Keeping your ideas simple
▶ Employing effective research
▶ 'Board-blasting'

Evaluating the competition

One of the first things to do is to look at the competition – that is, find out what other events seem to be popular at the moment. It may be that outdoor, challenge events – involving sponsored competitors in physical feats of endurance – are commonplace or that fundraising balls in unusual venues are proving successful. The trick is not to copy those ideas, for you will never be innovative that way, but rather to think of a different angle that might be taken with an already successful concept. As an innovative approach to the above examples, you might decide on a challenge event centred on Loch Ness or a fundraising ball on a Eurostar train.

Ideally, you need a concept for an event that includes at least one element that nobody has seen or heard of before, a concept so novel and exciting that your target audience will immediately clear their diaries for the date and be inspired to donate considerable sums of money to your cause. You should, of course, also consider what your potential audience is looking for, what will provide the unique hook. Remember that all events should enable people to have a good time because when people are enjoying themselves they are much more likely to give to charity.

When the famous concert promoter Harvey Goldsmith first approached the British Red Cross about a show to help victims of landmines, he talked about asking his many pop and rock group contacts to perform. But of course it had been done before, from Live Aid to the Simple Truth concert, so he started to consider alternatives that had not been tried before.

Goldsmith came upon the idea of a dance concert – after all, dancers are dependent on the use of their limbs, and many landmine survivors lose their own limbs, so there was a very natural and emotive link there. By taking that concept, inviting the cream of the dance world to perform, and promoting the message of landmines heavily at the concert, he created an extremely popular and successful show.

Keeping your ideas simple

In essence, a successful event must be marketable, saleable and profitable. Innovation will give an edge to your event that other 'traditional' offerings may lack. What you do not want is to think up such a complicated concept, however creative, that it simply confuses the public. The best and most popular ideas are often the simplest. You will probably need to promote your event through the media, on posters, and using other avenues to reach your potential audience, so find an event concept that is easy for people to grasp.

On a local basis, Macmillan Cancer Relief had been successfully raising funds through coffee mornings for many years. When one county decided to coordinate its various coffee mornings so that they all took place on the same day, public and media interest was increased. Building on this success, Macmillan decided to coordinate its coffee mornings across the whole country, branding the events part of 'The World's Biggest Coffee Morning'. With a set day in October each year, a more attractive and marketable national promotion began to take shape.

Today, Macmillan's coffee mornings are run by thousands of fundraisers across the UK, with events taking place anywhere from village halls and stately homes to shopping centres and even Heathrow Airport. This localised approach with national backing, essentially putting a spin on a very traditional fundraising event and making it special, now raises over £2 million annually and receives major sponsorship from Nescafé.

If you have a novel idea for an event which you would like to run nationally, but you are not sure how well it will work, it may be worth piloting it at a local or regional level first. You can then tinker with various elements of the event until you hit upon the right formula, but without losing too much money if it flops as local events are often cheaper to organise. It also limits the risk of adverse publicity if things do not run to plan. Similarly, if your event is to be regional, you could still pilot it on a reduced scale.

Employing effective research

As in most aspects of event organisation, thorough research is key, in this case to finding a new and exciting concept. It is worth staying well informed about developments in the arts world and entertainment field if you want to find the 'next big thing' and use it at your next event. Try to find someone who is planning to attend a major festival, like the Edinburgh Festival or the Eisteddfodd, and ask them to report back on interesting new acts. If you do not know anyone who is going, think about asking a colleague to attend or going yourself.

If visiting festivals is too expensive or impractical, check out popular listings magazines such as *Time Out*, *What's On* and *Heat*. These are often available in libraries, or alternatively you might consider taking out a subscription as they contain a great deal of information on developments in the performing arts, details of exciting new venues, and plenty of other ideas for the discerning events organiser. The Internet has now also become a valuable source of this information; typing 'entertainment', or 'entertainment listings' will reveal dozens of useful links.

This sort of research is worthwhile, as it can suggest the unique spin which will turn a 'so-so' event into a 'must' for your audience. The Walt Disney Company's premiere for the film *Mulan* included a live set from the Chinese State Circus and a balcony performance by popular violinist Vanessa Mae, which took the premiere out of the ordinary.

Several years ago, one small but enterprising charity pursued the rights to *Endurance*, a Japanese challenge game-show that shot to fame on British TV on *The Clive James Show*. The charity tracked the UK rights to a management agency and began negotiations. Unfortunately, the rights were too expensive, but the charity had been the first to approach the agency, even before any commercial enquirers. With sponsorship backing it might have finalised the deal and been the envy of other UK charities.

An important piece of advice here: if you succeed in coming up with a truly innovative concept for an event, and you think it could become an annual event for your charity, you should consider protecting it under copyright or patent. This will prevent other organisations – be they charities or commercial companies – copying your idea and perhaps weakening its impact in successive years. Major regular events, like Charity Project's Red Nose Day, are protected by copyright, and it need not cost much for you to follow suit and safeguard your future income. The Patent Office (see *Resources*) can provide more details.

'Board-blasting'

Bring together some committee members and key colleagues early one evening. Have a flip chart ready, appoint a chairperson, give everyone a glass of wine – and ask for any ideas for your forthcoming event.

Creativity often comes when people are feeling relaxed; it is surprising what novel ideas will be suggested when people are brought together informally and without any pressure. Throw in your own ideas on possible themes, suggest some crazy concepts, get people thinking about unusual venues, and encourage everyone to share their thoughts. Keep the atmosphere friendly and avoid any comments like 'What a stupid idea!' or 'That wouldn't work.'

You may end up with over 100 ideas – you should certainly have no fewer than 30 after an hour or so. Whittle these down to the 10 best ideas, then go away and develop them in more detail. Who knows what original event you may end up with. Many successful fundraising activities over the years have had their genesis in board-blasting sessions. Board-blasting also makes sure volunteers and colleagues will jointly own whatever concept is finally decided upon, ensuring their vital support in the later stages of organising the event.

Checklist for innovation in action:

- Identify currently successful events.
- Keep your concepts simple.
- Research the entertainment world.
- Hold a board-blast session.
- Pilot new ideas on a small, local level.
- Protect new ideas through copyright or patent law.

CASE STUDY

Carluccio white truffle evening for the Terrence Higgins Trust

Fundraising consultant Lyndall Stein spent several years as director of fundraising at the Terrence Higgins Trust (THT). She outlines an innovative and very successful event held during her time there.

Any event has the potential to be affected, influenced and inspired by our own individual quirks, passions and interests. This can sometimes be dangerous: an event around a favourite figure who may be nobody else's favourite; a theme that may appeal only to you; a budget decision that is based on a passion for a particular performer, rather than a clear understanding of what the return on investment will be. Occasionally, personal interest can make an interesting link that is useful for the organisation.

My secret passion is wild mushrooms and of all THT's well-known supporters, what excited me most was when Antonio Carluccio became a member of the Three Hundred Club, our first big gift club. He is one of the world experts on wild mushrooms and a famous chef.

On occasion over the years I met him and declared my passion for both his culinary skills and mushrooms. He eventually offered to arrange a special mushroom event for us – a private dinner during the white truffle season.

In October of that year, we had a private dinner for about 15 people, featuring white truffles (which sell at about £800 a kilo). The event was a very individual and intimate occasion, to which we decided to invite only a small group of people who would have a lot to say to one another and who had a deep commitment to the trust. This was also to be an opportunity to talk to those special supporters who would be able to make a very significant contribution. We could offer them the opportunity to talk privately and sensitively not only to each other but also to our chief executive, Nick Partridge.

The essence of our Carluccio white truffle evening was this sensitive exclusivity. We already thought we would have a successful event when Elton John agreed to come to the dinner. The comedian Stephen Fry then consented to host the evening and used his humour and intelligence to great effect.

Chief Executive Nick Partridge was the only member of staff present at dinner. I and two of my fundraising colleagues kept in touch during the evening by mingling during the drinks and joining some of the guests for coffee. We also ensured that appropriate requests for further support were being made, with donation forms available if required.

The combination of the mushrooms, THT, Stephen Fry and Elton John attracted an amazing group of people, including George Michael and Mick Hucknall, some of whom we had never been able to have face-to-face conversations with before. The select nature of the event meant, sadly, that we had to turn many people away.

It was a highly successful evening. As expected, Stephen Fry had everyone laughing. Tony Whitehead, one of our long-time volunteers, a founder of the organisation and a person living with AIDS, talked movingly about the epidemic, and Nick Partridge made a clear request for future support.

It was an event that enabled us to focus on developing relationships, and by its end we had generated gifts of almost £500,000. Sadly, I didn't get to eat any mushrooms.

Lessons learned:

- A simple concept made the event easy to sell to potential guests.
- Intimate surroundings suited the mood of the event.
- Guests were asked directly to give money to the cause.

CASE STUDY

The British Red Cross Pot of Gold appeal

When both war and famine struck Somalia in 1992, the British Red Cross was already considering the opportunities for a fundraising appeal to support the work of the Red Cross in the field. But it was a phone call from Hereford that really set things going. A widow of 82 had walked into a British Red Cross shop and donated her wedding ring for Somalia. This frail old woman had seen the terrible pictures on television, but having no spare money, she gave her wedding ring instead.

Touched by the story, the British Red Cross believed that an appeal for jewellery had the potential to reach young and old, rich and poor alike. It was particularly appropriate to Somalia, where women wear gold jewellery as security against bad times. By the summer of 1992 most Somali women had sold their jewellery to buy food for their families – they had nothing left.

A name for the appeal was quickly agreed – the Pot of Gold – but a system was needed to collect and sell the jewellery. The British Red Cross was put in touch with Phillips, the auctioneers, who agreed to help with the appeal. They would receive all the jewellery collected and sort it out into different price ranges. Pieces worth £500 or more would be put into a major auction to be held at a London hotel that December, while less valuable pieces could be sold through Phillips' regional auction houses. The remainder would either be melted down for scrap or sold off as costume jewellery.

It was decided to appeal for jewellery in two main ways. To begin with, a committee of wealthy people would be established, who would each give a piece of their own jewellery, then persuade their own friends to contribute. Second, a public appeal would be launched through the media. Because the appeal was slightly unusual, the strategy was to obtain media coverage through the use of celebrities. It was also hoped to attract press attention with some of the items themselves, either because they were beautiful or out of the ordinary, or because the story behind them was particularly poignant.

Unfortunately, both the public appeal and the organising committee made a slow start. One attempt at a public launch using the model Iman failed, and the committee also struggled to function, unable to attract a chairperson of significant stature to persuade a large number of other wealthy people to join. The auction was subsequently delayed for three months until Valentine's Day the following year. This allowed press coverage to pick up. The actor Peter Egan took a keen interest in the appeal and agreed to go on television to promote it. His appearance resulted in the singer Sinead O'Connor agreeing to donate her Hollywood home to the appeal!

Tickets for the auction at the Savoy Hotel cost £20 each. The evening began with a champagne reception and simultaneous viewing, so the auction itself was turned into a major special event. Five hundred people attended on the night, which allowing for a few complimentary tickets generated £8,400 in revenue. People who were unable to attend but wanted to help donated a further £11,261.

The auction was a tremendous success. There were 148 items on offer, and every single one was sold. Almost every piece made more than its estimated price. In total the auction grossed £150,000 with costs at around £25,000, or 16%. Phillips' regional auctions also generated revenue, so that in the end over £200,000 was raised directly from the sale of the jewellery. Other contributions, including that from Sinead O'Connor, enabled the Pot of Gold appeal to raise a total of £1.3 million.

Lessons learned:
- Initial concept suggested by the actions of a member of the public.
- Celebrity support helped to raise awareness of the event.

3

Getting the budget right

Any event will always include an element of financial risk to the organiser. As a charity or not-for-profit organisation, you will have a clear duty to protect donors' money and to maximise your financial returns from investments you may make. In all but the most exceptional of circumstances, you should try to ensure that your event will at least cover its costs, if not make a profit for your organisation.

That means having a clear budget from the outset, one in which you have included all possible areas of expense, as well as all likely income. Remember that events can be very expensive to organise and financial controls are therefore very important. Depending on the size of your event, you may want an accountant or other financial expert to take an objective look at your draft budget, but you do not have to be a gifted mathematician to get the basics right.

This chapter will cover the following topics:
- ▶ Fixed and variable costs
- ▶ Predicting the income
- ▶ The break-even point
- ▶ Tax considerations

Fixed and variable costs

When constructing your event budget, the obvious place to start is with the fixed expenditure. This is likely to include the cost of hiring a venue and any ancillary costs attached to that, such as heating, insurance or the hiring of on-site staff. Also included here will be the costs of any entertainment you may be providing, such as a band, comedians, or an after-dinner speaker. These will remain the same no matter how many people attend the event.

Hidden costs should not be overlooked. If you have paid staff or regular volunteers who will be working on the organisation and promotion of an event, then you must include the cost of their time when drawing up the budget. If a member of staff earns £250 a week and spends two months working on an event, that is a cost of £2,000 on the event budget. The fact that you would be paying that member of staff anyway does not matter, for there is an 'opportunity cost' – the cost of the time they could have spent doing something else – involved in any task that a staff member undertakes. Any overheads that can be attached to the event should also be included in the budget at this stage. This might include a percentage of your regular office overheads or the extra costs incurred in keeping your office open for longer hours than normal, incurring heating, electricity and perhaps additional telephone costs.

Next you should think about the variable costs, most of which will revolve around the number of people who eventually attend your event. If you are providing food and drink for guests, then the total cost of this will clearly increase for each person who attends. So too might the cost of other facilities, such as toilets if the venue is without them. Fifty people might require five 'portaloos', 200 people will probably need 20, so again the costs will rise as the number of people attending your event increases.

It is critically important that any fixed costs outlined in your budget are not allowed to rise, as this will affect your calculations later on. You should also ensure that variable costs per person do not increase unduly. Make certain that all of your staff working on the event are aware of the budget implications. Limit the number of people who are allowed to authorise expenditure, and make sure that just one person monitors overall expenditure against budget. Alternatively, you might set up a control group, including yourself, your financial manager, and perhaps one or more trustees to monitor the progress of your event against the original plan and budget. A control group might only need to meet on a fortnightly basis, but its input and oversight is invaluable. Never allow your volunteers, however well meaning, to control your budgetary decisions.

Predicting the income

It is not enough to simply say that a special event will raise awareness. That may be true, but raising awareness is only ever the means to another end. Any event, if well organised, can provide opportunities to raise money, either directly at the event itself or in the weeks and months that follow. If your event requires people to buy tickets to attend, then you have your first income stream right there but, as with some of the costs, this is clearly a variable figure, dependent on how many tickets are sold.

The event may also feature a raffle, or even an auction, and again you should attempt to predict income from these and build it into your budget. Be conservative, and remember that likely income will usually increase in proportion to the number of guests. If this is your first event, and you have no benchmark from which to start, then find a friendly contact in another charity with more experience, and ask them for an estimate of how much money you might expect to make through your activities.

Sponsorship is another avenue you might consider, either approaching a large donor to underwrite the entire cost of the event or getting smaller donors to pay for certain elements like the food, wine, or decorations. Sponsorship opportunities are examined in detail in *Chapter 4*, but if you are reasonably confident of attracting funds in this way include them in your budget.

If you intend to raise money through your event, there are various laws you should be aware of. It is important to remember that any game of chance, such as a raffle or tombola, is covered by the 1976 Lotteries and Amusement Act, and you will need to ensure that it is legal under this act. Depending on your likely annual turnover from such games, you will need to register with either the licensing section of your local council or the Gaming Board for Great Britain (see *Resources*). The Gaming Board for Great Britain's free leaflet 'Lotteries and the Law' can tell you more.

If your event is to feature live entertainment like dance, music or other performance, you might consider recording the event for future sales on music CD or video. Several charities have done this with gala concerts and shows and have found that the income from sales can vastly exceed any money taken on the night itself. However, if you are planning to hold such an event, you will need to consider performance rights that may be payable to the original writers of music or drama. You may also need to obtain a public entertainment licence from the licensing section of the local council. The venue owner or local council can advise you here.

The break-even point

Having set out your likely costs and income, you must decide whether to proceed. You need to consider your return on investment, often called the ROI. For example, if you expect to raise £10,000 from your event on costs of £3,000, then every pound spent is returning £3.33 in income, giving an ROI of 1:3.3. If, however, you know that a public collection will cost £500 and raise £2,500 – resulting in an ROI of 1:5 – then it may not make sense to proceed with the event. Of course, the event may not be a fundraiser, or you may be keen to attract new supporters who will give even more money to your charity in the future. Many large charities may even make a small loss to recruit new supporters if they feel a substantial profit can be made in a few years. You will need to think carefully about these issues, as will your trustees.

When considering income from your event, you should be looking at net income, that is the money you will make once all costs have been covered. Some organisations still judge their events, and indeed other fundraising activities, on the basis of gross income, but as they never see all of that money, it is an accounting method of which professional auditors would not approve.

Be especially critical of any financial risk you are taking. For example, do you have to place a non-refundable deposit on the venue several months before the event? Is there any other expenditure you need to commit to before you have begun properly marketing the event?

To help analyse the potential financial risk of the event, you will need to determine what your break-even point will be, looking in particular at your variable costs and income streams. Let us assume that fixed costs on your event total £5,000, with variable costs at £6 per person. Let us also assume that tickets to your event cost £15 and you reasonably expect to make a further £5 per person by selling raffle tickets or a programme for the event.

You can see that 100 guests will cost you £5,600 and generate income of £2,000. Increase the predicted number of guests to 300, and you have costs of £6,800 and forecast income of £6,000. You are almost at the break-even point. Increase the number of guests to 360, and costs become £7,160 against income of £7,200. You are now in profit. In fact, 358 is the number of guests at which forecast income exceeds anticipated costs, so that would be the break-even point. Further examples of sample budgets – one for an event destined to lose money and one for an event likely to turn a profit – are given in the box opposite.

You need to be sure that you can attract the number of guests required to reach the break-even point. Even if you are sure, you should try to arrange for most of the fixed costs, particularly the rental of the venue, to be deferred until well into the marketing of the event when you should have a clearer idea of how ticket sales are going. If you have to confirm the venue two months before the event, and by that point you have only sold 30 tickets, think very carefully about whether to proceed. Do not ever be afraid to cancel an event if necessary, for it is far better to do so than to lose charitable funds on a failed event; your trustees have a legal duty to protect the funds of your charity. Sponsorship can help to alleviate some of these risks – make sure it is agreed in writing – but you will still need to consider whether pursuing the event is an appropriate use of your sponsor's money.

Sample budgets

	The loss-maker	The profit-maker
	100 people attending	300 people attending
Fixed costs		
Hire of venue	£600	£1,200
Catering facilities	£250	£400
Staff time	£500	£1,500
Advertising and publicity	£150	£200
Entertainment	£100	£150
Variable costs		
Food/drink (per person)	£10	£15
Total costs	**£2,600**	**£7,950**
Fixed income		
Sponsorship	(n/a)	£1,000
Variable income		
Ticket sales (per person)	£15	£20
Raffle (per person)	£3	£3
Auction (per person)	(n/a)	£10
Total income	**£1,800**	**£10,900**
Profit/(loss)	**(£800)**	**£2,950**

When the National Trust was running its Snowdon Appeal, to raise money to buy the famous Welsh landmark, it considered holding a fundraising concert in Cardiff. Various Welsh artists, such as Manic Street Preachers, Shirley Bassey and opera stars, were approached and the office of HRH The Prince of Wales indicated that he might be free to attend that night.

However, the proposed date for the concert was just eight weeks away, and the fixed costs of hiring the venue meant that 80% of tickets would need to be sold before the event could break-even. When a number of the top stars discovered they were unable to perform that night, the trust had to decide if the concert was worth the financial risk and the potential embarrassment of having a major royal figure present at a half-full concert. The trust decided not to go ahead with the event: the Snowdon Appeal still went on to reach its target.

Tax considerations

Once you are sure that your event will make money, you need to decide how best to process that income. From the Charity Commission's point of view, fundraising itself can never be a genuine 'charitable object', and that means the profits from any event are potentially liable to direct taxation. There are some exceptions to this rule. Under the Inland Revenue's Extra Statutory Concession C4, events such as bazaars, jumble sales, gymkhanas, carnivals, fireworks displays and similar activities are exempt from corporation tax, provided:

- the event is not held regularly, i.e. it happens less than four times a year in the same locality;
- it does not compete with other 'traders';
- those people attending the event are aware that profits are going to charity; and
- profits from the event are transferred to charity or otherwise applied for charitable purposes.

This concession will, however, only apply to events that are small in scale, so the majority of large-scale special events are unlikely to be covered by this exemption. In assessing the size of an event, the Inland Revenue will consider the degree of commercial organisation involved (including the input of professional organisers and celebrities), the number of people attending, and the levels of turnover and profit from the event.

If your event is intended primarily to promote a campaign or to raise awareness of your organisation's activities – with the fundraising aspects very much secondary objectives – then any income generated by the event may be tax-exempt. This will be the case if the event is deemed to be contributing to a 'primary purpose' of the charity, as income from 'primary purpose' activities is generally not liable to direct tax. For example, if you are a health education charity and your event will promote the benefits of a healthy diet, that may be considered a 'primary purpose' activity. In any case, it is always prudent to take advice from the Inland Revenue at the earliest opportunity when planning your event, although in some cases you may not be given a definitive answer until after it has taken place.

If you know that your event income will be subject to corporation tax, or if you are simply not sure, the safest route is to run your event through a trading subsidiary of your charity (usually a subsidiary company wholly owned by the charity). These subsidiary companies allow charities to undertake a whole range of trading activities, from organising events through to running high street shops and selling Christmas cards. The company normally pays its trading profits back to the charity on an annual basis through a deed of covenant, thereby allowing the charity to claim back the corporation tax from the Inland Revenue.

Most of the biggest charities, and indeed many smaller ones, have already established trading subsidiaries. If you have not, and if you expect to be running large-scale events regularly or undertaking any other trading activity, it is well worth setting up such a company. This will, however, be dependent on your charity's constitution, and you should always seek professional advice. Sources of additional information on this topic can be found under *Further reading*.

Checklist for getting the budget right:

- Consider all potential costs.
- Include hidden costs (e.g. staff time).
- Impose financial controls on expenditure.
- Include various fundraising opportunities during event.
- Approach potential sponsors.
- Calculate the break-even point.
- Seek professional advice on tax implications for income and expenditure.

CASE STUDY

The Royal British Legion's Millennium Poppy Ball

The Royal British Legion planned a Millennium Poppy Ball in April 1999 to launch the legion's celebrations of the Millennium, which would lead up to its 80th birthday celebrations in 2001. This was to be the first major ball organised by the legion since its Great VE-Day Party in 1994.

The primary objective of the poppy ball was not to raise funds, but to raise awareness of the important work of the Royal British Legion – namely, that it offers financial, social and emotional support to one in four of the UK population, a total of some 15 million ex-service men and women and their dependants. A secondary aim was to increase the number of high-level supporters of the organisation. In keeping with the exclusive nature of the ball, the event was limited to 400 guests.

While the event did not set out to make money, the organisation insisted that it be run on a sound financial basis. The ball needed to be of a very high standard to compete successfully with many other pre-Millennium events, and expenditure was likely to be high. It was therefore decided to proceed only if sufficient sponsorship could be secured.

The fixed costs for the event were as follows:

Venue Natural History Museum	£11,600
Production lighting and sound	£15,000
Photography	£500
Theming Floral decorations, flags (some provided at discount or sponsored)	£5,300
Entertainment Singer and piano, dance band, table entertainers, toastmaster	£6,200
Printing Application forms, admission cards, menu cards, souvenir programme (partly sponsored by printer)	£7,300
Transport for volunteers and celebrities	£250
Complimentary tickets x 30 at £94.50 each	£2,835
Total fixed costs	**£48,985**

Sponsorship from British Energy and BT Defence more than covered this amount, with each company committing £25,000. Variable costs were then worked out as outlined below:

Table gifts for ladies	@ £3 per person
Table gifts for men (part sponsored)	@ £1.50 per person
Catering: food and drink, table settings, staff and transport	@ £90 per person
Furniture hire: table and chairs	@ £3 per person
Total variable costs per person	**£94.50**

Tickets were priced at £150 per person, so the legion was sure of a profit, after variable costs, of £55.50 per person. The event went ahead, and with further fundraising activities on the night, including a raffle and an auction, along with the sale of advertising space in the event programme, the ball raised a total of £145,000 gross income. Once all costs had been deducted, £65,000 was left as net income for the Royal British Legion's funds.

Lessons learned:

- Huge expenditure essential to success, so sponsorship vital.
- Ticket prices exceeding costs guaranteed a profit.

4

Attracting funders

As mentioned in *Chapter 3*, generating net income from events should never be overlooked, even if you simply plan to raise awareness of your cause or campaign. Donors are able not only to provide important resources for your future work, they can also go a long way towards underwriting the actual costs of running the event.

This chapter will cover the following topics:

▶ Locating potential funders
▶ Creating a sponsorship package
▶ Making the approach
▶ The benefits to an event sponsor

Locating potential funders

Many charities will already have a number of existing individual or corporate donors they can ask to sponsor all or part of an event. Some of these may have even supported similar events in the past. When considering whom to approach, start with those who have annually donated above average amounts when compared with your other regular supporters. These big givers will have taken considerable interest in your work before and will have already shown themselves to have substantial financial resources. Never be afraid to ask them for further support, but do think through your approach before requesting a meeting with a potential sponsor.

Consider what aspects of your work the company or individual has supported in the past. If you are running an event to promote the need for conservation in a local wood, then a large donor who has supported conservation work in the past may well be interested in sponsoring the event. However, if your aim is to raise money to support your work, then you need to illustrate how sponsorship can act as a lever to generate more new donations, worth several times as much as the funds they are contributing. If you cannot demonstrate this, a donor may simply choose to give money directly to your cause rather than sponsor an event.

Think about approaching any commercial firms with existing links to your organisation, such as auditors, bankers, lawyers or printers. Few companies view their charity clients as just another account – they will usually take particular interest in your cause and many will be only too glad to repay your custom with financial support for an event.

> The Royal National Institute for the Blind (RNIB) runs a very successful annual wine tasting event in the City of London, with every element of the event sponsored. That sponsorship is generated thanks to a committee, chaired by RNIB's auditors, which comprises the charity's insurers, clearing bank, investment advisers and solicitors. The bank provides the venue, the investment firm looks after the catering, the auditors handle the marketing of the event to other City contacts, and a national off-licence chain donates the wine. This event now regularly raises almost £20,000 a year through ticket sales, an auction and other fundraising on the night.

As the RNIB example illustrates, gifts in kind can be extremely beneficial if supporters are unable to donate money to fund your event. What is more, companies that support you in this way can get pleasure out of giving and helping to raise funds in an extremely cost-effective way. Would the local newspaper where you place your recruitment advertising be prepared to advertise your next event free of charge? Or would your regular printer be prepared to print event tickets for free or at a discount? Or could a local florist provide flowers to decorate the tables at your dinner? Many charities find gifts in kind to be an extremely lucrative source of funding.

If you do not have an event committee, put one together as soon as possible for all but the smallest events because they can prove invaluable. Approach your existing contacts, whether they are supporters, commercial suppliers of goods or services to your charity, or family and social contacts. Committee members should certainly have an affinity with your cause, but also influential enough in their fields to attract further support for your event.

Committee members, or their business and social contacts, can be called upon to act as main event sponsors, as donors of essential items like food or flowers, or as advertisers in your event programme if you are producing one. Alternatively, you can ask committee members to serve as fundraisers, selling tickets to your event, or raffle or prize draw tickets if these additional activities are planned.

Creating a sponsorship package

If you are planning to find a sponsor for your event, think carefully about how you package the benefits to them. You must first decide if you are likely to attract a single sponsor for the whole event – which may entail giving exclusive rights to that supporter – or whether you will need to approach several sponsors to take on different elements.

To make this decision, you must know your marketplace. If your event is going to cost £10,000 to put on and your committee chairperson is also the managing director of a large company, there is a fair chance that the company might view £10,000 as a reasonable amount to spend for the publicity they will receive. If, however, your event is going to cost £5,000 and your contacts are small local retailers, sponsorship packages costing a few hundred pounds each would be more realistic.

Bear in mind that you may have to pay corporation tax on the income from any sponsorship package if it is not deemed to be a pure donation. Because a company may be considered to have received a 'commercial benefit' from supporting your event – essentially advertising for the company – sponsorship does not receive the same tax concessions as do regular donations. The sponsor may also have to pay VAT unless their contribution is considered a pure donation or they are linking their company to just a one-off event.

This is a rather complex area, and you should seek professional advice if possible. More detailed information can be found in some of the titles listed under *Further reading* at the end of this book. In essence, the Inland Revenue will regard reference to an event sponsor as an advertisement and will levy corporation tax on sponsorship income to the event organiser if the reference incorporates either:

- the sponsor's logo;
- the sponsor's corporate colours; or
- mention of the sponsor's products or services.

It is therefore advisable not to offer these benefits in any sponsorship package unless your event is being organised through a trading subsidiary, as outlined in *Chapter 3*.

In addition, a sponsor will have to pay VAT on its sponsorship if it receives either hospitality or exclusive/priority booking rights for the event. VAT can be avoided if the sponsor is prepared to take limited credit – for instance, simply being listed in the acknowledgements in the event programme. However, it is extremely unlikely that any company will agree to sponsor an event under those conditions, so be prepared to add the standard rate of VAT (currently 17.5%) to the cost of any sponsorship package.

The tax laws can also work in favour of your event and a potential sponsor's interests. If the sponsor's contribution is considered a pure donation and exceeds £100, it could be paid to your charity under the Gift Aid scheme. This may have tax advantages to the sponsor, as the gross amount – including any tax that would be payable on the donation – will become an allowable charge when calculating a company's corporation tax liabilities. So if a sponsor pays £1,000, they will save £400 in corporation tax at 40%.

Once you have set the sponsorship packages and their rates, it is important to stick to them. There is nothing more galling to a supporter than discovering that another company has received extra benefits in return for the same level of support. Companies talk to each other, through chambers of commerce, Rotary clubs and other groups, so do not think they will never find out. They will, which could considerably weaken support for your next event.

Making the approach

If approaching potential sponsors yourself would prove difficult, or you simply do not have the time, then call on your event committee for help. If your committee members cannot approach a potential supporter, then look for any other 'warm' contacts before you go in cold. Ensure that those making the approach have themselves donated something to the event. Indeed, a good event committee chairperson will insist on all committee members either donating or securing a gift for the event.

Using other contacts can also provide further benefits. For example, if you know someone who works for a certain company, ask them to take a proposal to their marketing department or managing director on your behalf. They need not be a senior member of staff themselves. This is likely to work better than if you make an approach unknown and unannounced.

Alternatively, if your event and its budget are both large enough, you could employ a sales agency to offer the sponsorship packages on your behalf. Not only will these companies relieve you of the time and effort of calling existing supporters, they may also be able to open doors to new supporters with whom you have had no previous contact. Experienced sales agencies have their own databases of companies and contacts that they approach on a regular basis.

If you are intending to use a sales agency, it is important to have a formal signed contract. Look carefully at the commission rate that agencies normally apply – it could be anywhere between 20% and 50% of gross income (if it is even higher than that, do not touch the agency). You will have to assess whether you want or can afford to employ an agency on that basis. Your budget may well be the determining factor because if the profit margin on the event is already slim, losing even a small part of your income in commissions to an agency may result in you forecasting a loss from the event.

If you are employing an agency to sell sponsorship, or even simply to sell advertising space in an event programme, pay special attention to the Charities Act 1993 (available from the Stationery Office, ISBN 010 541093 4, see *Resources*). Under this act, any third-party agency is likely to be viewed in law as a 'commercial participator' or 'professional fundraiser', that is, a for-profit company making money through services to charities or through an association with a charity. In such cases there must be a written agreement between your charity and the agency. The agency must also make a clear statement to any potential donors or sponsors informing them what proportion of their money will be passed on to the charity, and consequently what proportion the agency will retain by way of a fee.

While failure to comply with the act is technically an offence by the agency, you should ensure for your own peace of mind that the law is being obeyed. To do so, and to check that your own organisation is being properly represented to potential sponsors, ask to see any materials that are produced to sell the sponsorship packages, such as letters or brochures. If sponsorship is being offered over the telephone, then make sure you vet the script that the agency's tele-sales staff will use, and ask if you can listen in on some of the calls. Any reputable agency should agree to that.

Checklist for attracting funders:

- Approach existing donors first.
- Approach any commercial contacts (e.g. banks, solicitors).
- Ask for support as gifts in kind.
- Get committee members to approach their contacts.
- Design a comprehensive sponsorship package.
- Check for tax implications.
- Employ a sales agency if necessary, but check commission rates and the law first.

CASE STUDY

The National Trust and spring plant fairs

When the National Trust planned a series of spring plant fairs to be held simultaneously at 52 of its properties, it needed support from various quarters to make the event a success.

Gardening is among the principal interests of the majority of the National Trust's two-and-a-half million members, so the organisation knew it had a vast captive and receptive audience. As the trust owns its properties, it had few problems arranging venues. Where help was needed was in making money from the event.

Two thousand volunteers agreed to grow plants for the sales, and these were available alongside the stalls of commercial growers, who could sell their own produce in return for paying a fee to the trust. Raffles were also organised for the majority of properties, with prizes donated by garden suppliers, including lawnmower manufacturer Atco Qualcast. A booklet of garden tips was produced for sale, with sponsorship from the New Covent Garden Soup Company, keen to promote its use of fresh, high quality vegetables.

Raising awareness of the event was done in conjunction with appropriate media. *BBC Gardeners World* magazine ran a sales promotion with tickets to the event as a reward, while major free publicity was secured in the *Daily Telegraph*, whose readership closely matches the trust's typical membership profile. Posters and leaflets were also designed and displayed widely throughout the trust's properties.

The support of volunteers and commercial supporters enabled the event to raise a net income of more than £65,000, with gifts in kind valued at a further £60,000 used as raffle prizes and for free publicity. This success has since been repeated at two more national spring plant fairs, with the most recent attracting over 46,000 people and raising more than £71,000.

Lessons learned:
- Sponsorship minimised costs and risk to the organisation, maximising profits.
- Sponsors were asked for support appropriate to their business.
- Use of volunteers helped generate ownership of the events at trust properties.

5

Choosing venues

The most visible element of any event is the venue and as a result great care should be taken over its choice. A good venue will add value to your event, allowing you to attract more people and, depending on costs, achieve a higher income. Conversely, a bad venue can cause all manner of logistical headaches and may result in your target audience feeling that they have seen it all before, with a resulting drop in the number of people attending the event.

This chapter will cover the following topics:

▶ Identifying potential venues
▶ Checking out the venue
▶ Contracts and insurance
▶ Travelling to the venue
▶ Using a venue through a third party

Identifying potential venues

The perfect venue for your event could be anywhere. For a large-scale event, you could consider somewhere made famous through television, such as London's Royal Albert Hall, New York's Brooklyn Bridge, Edinburgh Castle (site of the famous annual tattoo), the Sydney Opera House or the Manchester Royal Exchange. Or it could be somewhere new, such as the Millennium Dome, which must now feature on many event organisers' wish lists, or maybe the Berlin Parliament building. For a smaller scale special event, it may be a popular theatre, or perhaps a well-known museum like the Yorvik Centre in York or the National Museum of Photography, Film and Television in Bradford.

With such a vast range of venues on offer, you will need to narrow your choices. In the early stages of planning your event, consider the type of audience you will be targeting, for that should help to determine what type of venue would be attractive to them. For instance, if you are organising a lunch for corporate contacts then you might consider using a private club or a mayoral residence. If the season is right, then a racecourse or greyhound track might help to lure businesspeople from their offices and boardrooms.

Think about what your likely audience would enjoy. If their idea of a good night out is food, drink and entertainment, maybe there is a novelty or themed pub nearby that would make an attractive and cost-effective venue. You can usually hire the whole or part of the premises for private events.

If you are arranging a summer ball or another event that will attract a large number of socially prominent people, consider a venue they may not have visited before. As the guest lists for this type of occasion tend to include the same people, top hotels are losing their appeal because many potential guests have been to them several times. Stately homes or museums are often a novel venue. Consider a castle or the official residence of a local or national dignitary, which may not normally be open to the public and will therefore provide an additional interest.

However, if your audience is likely to be younger and slightly less affluent, then a well-known night-club, concert hall or cinema may be a better choice. If the audience is to be made up of those under 30, why not consider an amusement or theme park, many of which are available for private hire?

The Australian Red Cross each year organises a Desperate and Dateless Ball for young, single people. This event is held in a theme park with lake, mock castle, cinema and dance hall – making it an event with varying styles of venue, all of which appeal to that particular audience.

You could also think about turning the venue on its head. If the activity you plan is typically held indoors, like chess for example, why not make it an outdoor event? Or take an outdoor event like cricket and create an indoor tournament. You might need to use a little lateral thinking here, but that will create the ideal hook for your potential audience.

Making an obvious link with your cause will also help, particularly when marketing the event to existing supporters. If your cause or organisation has a sporting theme, then a football ground or sports club may be appropriate, or maybe a country club or private estate where outdoor pursuits could be enjoyed. Of course, if you are raising funds for an institution like a hospital, museum or theatre, that institution itself could provide the perfect venue for any event. That would allow actual and potential donors to experience for themselves the value and grandeur of the cause they are supporting – and you to use a building where you will have rather more control.

Not all venues have to be ready made; a very dull and uninspiring building or location can be specially designed and dressed up to suit the occasion. A marquee, an abandoned warehouse, a factory or some other building can, with some expense and plenty of imagination, be transformed into the venue of your dreams. Within a simple shell, you can create a fantasyland, a period of history, or any other environment that you think will attract the right audience.

> The Walt Disney organisation, which holds parties after its film premieres, often uses marquees. Its party for the premiere of *Mulan* – a film set in China – involved six huge marquees with water gardens, oriental flowers and Chinese styled rooms, making it an evocative and highly successful event.

Remember, if you are transforming an existing building, particularly one that has been unused for some time, do take extra care to examine safety aspects before you begin planning the event. If you expect to do anything more than cosmetic decoration, it is worth checking building regulations with the owner of the property first.

Finding new and innovative venues which will excite your intended guests does take time, but it will be worth the effort. That essential tool, research, is vitally important here. Some celebrities own fantastic homes that could be used, so keep scanning the local media to discover if any celebrities live in or close to the area where you hope to hold your event.

Of course, it is always a good idea to build strong links with any influential people who live near to your headquarters or local offices and whom you feel might help your cause. Invite them to your events, ask them to serve on committees, get them to visit your projects or work, and then when you need to ask for their support, they should feel suitably motivated to help (*Chapter 6* will look at this area in more detail). Their previous involvement may mean that they are more likely to loan their home to you for a fundraising party.

Checking out the venue

Always visit any venue before you book it, even if you have used it before, as decorative and structural changes may have been made since you were last there. Before you go, work out all the different elements you will need for your event, and at the venue try to visualise them all in place. Consider practical issues, for example, if there is a stage, is it large enough for your purposes or can it be extended? Think about the height of the rooms – a cavernous space can often ruin the atmosphere of a small-scale or even large-scale event, and tall ceilings are extremely difficult to hang banners or balloons from. Lighting and decoration are also important considerations.

Check if the venue is going to be large enough for the anticipated number of guests. If you are planning a sit-down event, perhaps with food and entertainment, make sure the room is big enough to allow everyone to see the main activities, for there is nothing worse than seating some guests in remote overflow rooms, where they inevitably feel removed from the excitement.

You should pay particular attention to access and facilities for the disabled. While newly constructed venues should have the very latest facilities to comply with the law, older buildings, particularly stately homes with their lack of ramps and lifts, may create terrible problems for any disabled guests. If your event is open to all, then you must ensure the venue caters for all. It is too late to think about these issues on the night, when a wheelchair-bound guest arrives at the door. Take advice from the local council or a disability awareness group if you are unsure, and consult the 1995 Disability Discrimination Act and Code of Practice, or the DDA Helpline (see *Further reading* and *Resources*).

If you are not the first organisation to use the venue, try to talk to someone who has organised an event there in the past. The owner should be happy to put you in touch with them – if they are not, then beware as they almost certainly have something to hide. However carefully you check the venue, there is nothing like practical experience to flush out any idiosyncrasies or hidden problems, so if someone has used it before, get the benefit of their experience.

Contracts and insurance

Once you are sure you have found the perfect venue, you will naturally want to book it, but first check the terms of the contract you are about to sign. No one can predict how the marketing of an event will go, and if at any stage you need to scrap the event, perhaps because of poor ticket sales, there is sure to be a penalty fee when you cancel the venue booking. Insurance can be arranged for most events, which can cover any such cancellation fees. While sometimes expensive, it may be worth considering, particularly if the penalty is large.

When booking a venue, make sure you are completely clear about what you will be getting. If you are using a stately home, for example, you might find that some basic facilities are not available and will need to be ordered and paid for separately. You might discover there is no central heating system, no working kitchen or galley, or not enough toilets to cater for the number of guests expected at your event. Portable toilets are extremely expensive to hire.

Before confirming the booking, always find out when you will get access to the venue. If you are holding an evening event, and the premises are open to the general public during the day, or being used for another event, you may not be allowed in until the early evening. If so, unless certain rooms are available in advance, you may find you simply do not have the time to prepare everything before your guests are due to arrive.

Travelling to the venue

Naturally, you will want your guests to get to the venue easily and to arrive there in style. If your event or venue is truly unique, you may well find people are willing to come from hundreds of miles away. If you are expecting this, it may be worth investigating whether overnight accommodation is available at, or close to, your venue. Hotels are often happy to give special charity rates, particularly outside the holiday season. In normal circumstances, somewhere between 50 and 70 miles is probably the maximum distance you could expect people to travel to an event without wanting to stay overnight.

Whatever the distance, do make sure that your venue is easy to reach, either by motorway or major road, or by convenient rail links or bus routes. If not, you may need to provide a shuttle bus or coach to transport guests between a specified arrival point and the venue itself. If guests are likely to be driving, check that sufficient car parking spaces are available, or could be created without too much fuss. Make sure the car park is not a boggy field; just imagine the mud streaked guests and mired cars you would have to deal with in the rain.

One well-known public figure tells the story of a time when he and his wife spent £500 to attend a charity event consisting of a polo match followed by a gala dinner. On the day there were heavy thunderstorms and rain, which meant the polo match had to be called off. The dinner went ahead, however, but guests had to walk across a muddy field to get to the marquee where it was taking place. The occasion was a disaster, as the organisers had made no provision for the rain and were left watching helpless as women slipped in the mud in their best ball gowns. The impression left on the guests can be imagined; that particular individual has said he will never again attend an event organised by the charity concerned.

If you are expecting hundreds of cars, it is best to inform the police, who will need to consider the impact on regular traffic in the area. The AA or RAC can also provide special road signs for events of sufficient size, but they do need at least eight weeks notice for these, and both organisations charge a fee for the service (see *Resources*).

Some venues may come with their own special restrictions. If the venue is near to a residential area, limits on noise levels may be imposed, and the event might need to conclude by a set time – even Wembley Arena has to end its concerts by 10.30 at night for the sake of local residents. If you are planning a firework display, and your venue is within three miles of an aerodrome or airport, or beneath a recognised air traffic route, restrictions may also apply. The Airspace

Utilisation Section of the Civil Aviation Authority can provide more information (see *Resources*). Such a problem was faced by one charity a few years ago, when it planned a major firework display to end an event at Hampton Court Palace. The display had to be rescheduled to an earlier time for the benefit of local residents and the safety of those flying in and out of Heathrow Airport. No one had checked the rules and regulations in advance.

Unpredictable as the British weather may be, do consider the time of year when selecting your venue. An outdoor location may be ideal for the spring or summer months and even into early autumn with some luck, but holding an event in a marquee or at a sports ground in the depths of winter is usually unwise. It could cost you dearly if audiences stay away or, even worse, the event has to be cancelled. Some organisations do hold outdoor events in the winter, but most will take out bad weather insurance in case of cancellation to protect their charitable funds.

Using a venue through a third party

If you cannot get access to an appropriate venue yourself, consider linking with an organisation that can. Many clubs and societies, such as the Rotarians, the Lions, Soroptimists and professional societies, organise annual dinners and functions, often at prestigious venues. Most will run their events in aid of a charity, so it is worth approaching your local clubs to secure their patronage. Ask at local hotels to find out which organisations host balls or dinners and the time of year when they tend to take place. Cheque presentations, usually featured in local newspapers, can also alert you to the charitably minded organisations in your area.

These so-called piggy-back events can vary widely in terms of the involvement and work you may need to put in yourself. Some event organisers simply make a donation of any profit from the event, but others may expect you to help attract guests or to find a celebrity speaker. There may also be opportunities for you to provide your own promotional literature for guests, or to run a fundraising raffle or auction at the function itself.

For example, when Amnesty International wanted to mark the 50th anniversary of the International Declaration of Human Rights, it took a small travelling roadshow to many of Britain's top outdoor music festivals. This provided Amnesty with a captive audience of hundreds of thousands of teenagers and young adults – its exact target market for the campaign. Yet it reached this audience through relatively little work or organisation of its own.

If approached by a third party to participate in an event, clarify at the outset who will carry the financial risk and put everything in writing. Make sure that the style of event is suitable to your organisation – for example, if someone is organising a casino night and they want you to help out and benefit, does this conflict with any policies your organisation has on gambling or alcohol? Discuss the event in detail before making any commitment, and make sure you have full organisational support for any arrangements. You do not want to be taking all the responsibility if things go wrong.

Sharing an event with another charity can be beneficial, particularly if there is not much time for planning and organisation. That said, you are likely to be asked to provide volunteers and other assistance to the event, so be certain you can deliver what is requested.

Make sure that each side understands its responsibilities and is committed to the success of the event. Agree a split of any profits that reflects the work each side puts in. There is little point in organising 20 volunteers for an event that is only going to return £50 to your organisation – you would be better asking those volunteers to make collections in the local streets. Similarly, you do not want a 90:10 split in favour of the other party if you are sharing the workload equitably, although it might be worth taking 10% of the profits from an exclusive and profitable event which would otherwise be totally out of your reach.

Checklist for choosing a venue:

- Choose a venue that has added value.
- Visit the venue to picture the event in your mind.
- Work out what extra facilities you may need. Kitchens, toilets, etc. are not always provided.
- Consider the logistics of getting guests to and from the venue. Are there sufficient car parking spaces, public transport links, and accommodation?
- Watch out for special restrictions on the venue or its location.
- Check any contracts carefully before signing. In particular, look out for cancellation fees.
- Ask if there is a charity rate when booking your venue.
- Consider insuring your event, particularly if using an outdoor venue.

CASE STUDY

The British Red Cross, the QEII and the Orient Express

When P&O's flagship cruise liner the QEII was celebrating her 30th anniversary, the company offered the ship to the British Red Cross as the venue for a special event in aid of its anti-personnel landmine campaign, which was spearheaded by the late Diana, Princess of Wales.

The QEII was to be moored in Southampton harbour, and a unique day was planned for the paying guests. Those attending the luncheon would start their journey in London, from where they would take the Venice-Simplon Orient Express to Southampton, enjoying a full breakfast and a tour of the train on the way. On arrival at Southampton, they would be shown around the QEII before sitting down to a celebrity lunch with guest speakers.

The Princess of Wales herself was intending to be present, but her tragic death came just two months before. It was decided to proceed with the day in tribute to the princess, but one major sponsor withdrew their support.

There were some initial difficulties using this world-famous cruise liner, as the rooms originally earmarked for guests could not accommodate the numbers expected. In addition, the presentations were to take place in a lecture theatre in which a number of people would have to be seated with restricted views.

QEII officials were persuaded to move the opening reception to a different room, which, although less glamorous, could at least accommodate all the expected guests. The presentations were also moved into a lounge which could seat everyone once additional chairs were brought in. Extra chairs also had to be arranged for the dining room.

There were further problems on the day itself. A derailment outside London meant that many guests travelling from Waterloo Station would be more than 60 minutes late. This posed a number of difficulties, not least because Cherie Blair, wife of the prime minister, was to arrive at Southampton to greet the London train, but could only stay at the reception for 90 minutes before lunch.

On arrival, Cherie Blair agreed to circulate among the 150 guests who had arrived at Southampton by their own means. She was happy to meet and talk to them, and pose for official and unofficial photographs. She was very accommodating, but when we heard that the train from London was now running over 90 minutes late, Cherie Blair had to leave before it arrived at Southampton.

Fortunately, those guests on the Orient Express were not too concerned by the delays. Their party on the train had merely been prolonged. On arrival at Southampton, the guests had to miss the reception and instead went straight to the formal presentations.

In the lounge, Lord Attenborough, Elizabeth Dole (the then-president of the American Red Cross), and the chairman of the British Red Cross all paid tribute to Diana, Princess of Wales and commended the work she had done for victims of landmines. Guests were asked to support the British Red Cross Landmines programme. Despite the problems with venues and trains, and the lack of a major sponsor to cover the substantial costs, the day on the QEII and the Orient Express raised more than £50,000.

Lessons learned:

- Venue was adapted to accommodate the expected guests.
- Event schedule was flexible enough to amend in an emergency.

CASE STUDY

Macmillan Cancer Relief
Brixton prison sleepover

Brixton prison has had a long association with Macmillan Cancer Relief, with staff and inmates regularly fundraising for the charity, and Macmillan placing work with some of the prison's in-house businesses. When a wing of the prison was refurbished and about to be re-opened, Macmillan suggested a seminar on penal matters to promote greater understanding of the criminal justice system and a sponsored overnight sleep-in at the prison itself.

Those people taking part would arrive at Brixton prison in the evening, where they would hear presentations about the work of the prison and the work of Macmillan Cancer Relief. They would then be fed a basic prison meal and escorted to their cells, where they would be locked in overnight. Further information on Macmillan's work was to be left in each cell for the occupants to read at their leisure.

The charity targeted individuals from the legal profession, such as judges, magistrates and solicitors, as well as existing high-value donors. In addition, several high-profile and appropriate celebrities were invited, including the Home Secretary Jack Straw. As the event coincided with the Labour Party conference, the latter was unable to accept the invitation, but Shadow Home Secretary Michael Howard was only too pleased to attend in his place.

The charity aimed to raise just £5,000 from the event, which had very low costs. Prison service suppliers donated the food, and officers gave their time free. The attendance of individuals such as Michael Howard generated tremendous publicity, and the unique opportunity to stay at the prison did the rest. The event was heavily oversubscribed, and those who did take part raised over £90,000 through sponsorship.

Lessons learned:
- Theme of the event was appropriate to venue and targeted guests.
- Costs at the venue were kept to a bare minimum.
- The charity and supporter both got their messages across to guests.

6

Recruiting celebrity patrons

For many years, patronage revolved solely around the members of the royal family. Certainly, both the major and the minor royals have always been seen as extremely valuable supporters of any charitable cause, attracting other donors to both large and small charities. However, while the royal family was happy to appear on charitable letterheads and to make visits to the work of their chosen causes, most members were very reluctant to get too involved in fundraising events or other promotions.

The involvement of the Prince of Wales in the events of his own charity, the Prince's Trust, the support of the Princess Royal – particularly for Save the Children – and the work of the late Diana, Princess of Wales, marked a change in the royal family's attitude towards charity events. Combined with the use of celebrities in such fundraising activities as Live Aid, Comic Relief and Children in Need, famous individuals are now frequently linked to events, and many charities are likely to have a national, or at least local, celebrity to help promote and endorse their work.

This chapter will cover the following topics:
▶ Selecting a suitable patron
▶ Asking for celebrity support
▶ Using your celebrity at the event

Selecting a suitable patron

The vast array of celebrity patrons that are now employed at charity events can make finding a suitable individual a bewildering task. One general assumption is that famous people will not turn out for smaller charities, but the reality is very different. The actress Maureen Lipman regularly helps out at a small arts centre in Muswell Hill, and TV film critic Barry Norman can be found helping schools and hospices in his local county of Hertfordshire.

Start by carefully checking your local and regional newspapers, listening to your local radio stations and watching regional TV. These media will often feature stories on celebrities who live locally to your cause, so note down any promising individuals who appear. If you have a friendly contact at the newspaper or radio station, they may then be able to put you in touch with the celebrity.

The broadcast media itself can generate some well-known individuals – such as newsreaders and weather presenters – with enough public pulling power to bring a greater audience to your event. Consider talking to newspaper editors, television and radio journalists or presenters, particularly from local stations, although some national figures may also support charities. Martyn Lewis, for example, is a regular host of the Charities Aid Foundation annual conference and also supports many charities in the fields of cancer care and youth work.

Some people in the media have their own special charities that they helped to establish and which they support almost exclusively. For instance, Esther Rantzen is very closely linked with Childline, and the actor and comedian Lenny Henry with Charity Projects and Comic Relief. But others are happy to support a range of charities and appear regularly at many different special events. Angela Rippon, for instance, supports both the British Red Cross and NCH Action for Children, while others, such as Clare Rayner, are happy to attend many charity events to help increase publicity.

Look out for celebrities or well-known figures who could benefit from an association with your cause. When one national charity held an event at the apartments of Lord Irving, the Lord Chancellor, who had been attacked in the media for spending thousands of pounds redecorating his rooms, it was the 13th charity to make use of the venue. At the time of the controversy, and keen to neutralise his bad press, Lord Irving made sure he was seen and photographed at every charitable function. The events held there were also very successful, as people were intrigued to see the notorious apartments for themselves.

Political figures of all colours are popular choices to support charities and their events. You might consider approaching anyone from your local mayor or mayoress and councillors, to MPs, MEPs and even past prime ministers, if they happen to live locally or empathise with your cause.

Asking for celebrity support

After your research has identified an individual whom you believe would make a suitable patron, you will need to approach them. In many instances, you may be unable to talk directly to the celebrity, but instead will have to correspond with their agent or PR representative. Send a brief letter to the celebrity's appointed contact, many of whom are listed in *Spotlight* (see *Resources*), explaining why you believe the celebrity suits your cause, what your charity does, and what you would initially like the celebrity to do for you. It is often advisable to offer a few ideas for their involvement, in case your first suggestion does not appeal to them.

What should you ask your chosen celebrity to do? Most people today want to do more than just lend their name to your event letterhead, although there are some individuals who can genuinely only offer that. Unless their name is particularly compelling and liable to open a substantial number of doors to other supporters or donors, you should ignore these people in favour of others with more time and energy to devote to your event.

Your chosen patron could write appeals for sponsorship or invitations to the event. Alternatively, they may prefer to chair your event committee, or a sub-committee – for instance, on publicity – or donate money or items for your event, especially if it includes a raffle or a fundraising auction.

Do not overlook the impact a well-known personality could make at the event itself if they are able to attend. If your celebrity supporter is to be present, ensure that your other key supporters and those who have helped to organise the event are introduced to them. It may even be worth arranging for a photographer to be present, with a copy of the photograph being sent to everyone as a thank-you after the event.

When sending any letter requesting support, never depend on a quick reply. Most celebrities will be unable to say 'yes' immediately, and in many instances their agreement will depend on what professional engagements they are undertaking at the time. Some celebrities see charity events as an extension of their professional engagements and expect to make money from them, so enquire early on if the celebrity will charge for a personal appearance.

> The British Red Cross was fortunate to build a long-term relationship with Jane Horrocks when she was still a relatively little-known actress and before she had come to major British public attention in her supporting role in the situation comedy *Absolutely Fabulous*. Horrocks agreed to endorse a number of events during the charity's 125th birthday campaign and also visited development projects overseas. Now she has achieved widespread international fame for her starring role in the film *Little Voice* and is also a committed supporter of the British Red Cross.

The best piece of advice with celebrities is to be patient. It is important to remember that they will not agree overnight to support your event. Like any area of fundraising and PR, you should be trying to build a long-term relationship with them. Ideally, you want to approach an actor, sports star, or television celebrity when they are just beginning to come into the public eye, so that you can nurture the relationship as they become more popular. Many charities today are looking for celebrities to endorse a whole range of activities, so once someone is regularly featured in the media, they will be inundated with charitable requests.

Using your celebrity at the event

Having secured the support of your celebrity patron, you are likely to want to introduce them to your other guests at the event. If so, ensure you brief the celebrity well in advance. They will need to know exactly what they are going to do. Are they to make a short speech, how many people are they to meet, are they to have a microphone on stage? It is likely that anyone famous will attract at least some media attention, so you will need to ensure there are volunteers or colleagues around to help manage any situation that might arise.

> There is a story about Yoko Ono, the widow of John Lennon, arriving at a charity event in New York and being mobbed not just by the crowd but by the media. She was so frightened that for a number of years she refused to do any other charity event. This situation arose because there was no forward planning or management on the day itself. Make sure your celebrity is happy and comfortable at all times. If they are not, then they may not want to help you again.

Sometimes celebrities known for a particular talent may want to do something different at the event. For example, a pop singer may not want to sing but may prefer to compere an event, or even just attend as a regular guest. Similarly, today some members of the royal family rather than just sit in the audience at a charity gala prefer to appear on stage at the end of the show to be seen publicly thanking the cast for their performance and support.

There is no one systematic approach to use with celebrities. The best advice is to have a conversation with the person concerned well in advance, and ask them what they would like to do and how they would like to be used. Never ask anyone to do too much in the first instance, but instead build their involvement up over several occasions until you have secured a good, confident relationship with that individual.

Checklist for making patronage work:

- Scan the regional news for local celebrities.
- Approach those working in the media for their support or contacts.
- Send a brief introductory letter to your selected celebrity.
- Consider what your patron will do for the event.
- Be patient – never ask for too much at first.
- Follow the top tips for celebrities.

Top tips for dealing with celebrities

1. Ensure the celebrity is always well briefed and always made to feel important when invited to an event.
2. Always closely look after a celebrity during the event. It is important to have a member of staff keeping an eye on them, making sure they stay happy at all times.
3. Always offer to pay basic expenses for a celebrity – send a car, make sure they are sent a cheque if they are driving themselves, give them the train ticket, or pay their airfare if they are going on an overseas visit. They may refuse to accept, but the offer should be there.
4. Saying thank-you is important, so pay particular attention to sending birthday cards, flowers, get well cards if appropriate, and generally keeping in touch by letter or phone.
5. Sometimes invite celebrities to important events but do not ask them to do anything. Their presence at an annual meeting, at a celebration party, or even just going to see some of your work without any fuss or bother is often much appreciated by everyone concerned.
6. Involve celebrities in your planning decisions. Ask them what they would like to do – do not feel you always have to give them orders.
7. Keep on the right side of secretaries, personal assistants, or partners. Celebrities rarely manage their own diaries entirely by themselves, and if you need a favour you will often ask their assistant first. Their support is vital in getting the response you want.
8. Do not pay too much attention to fickle public interest. Today's celebrity may be tomorrow's 'has-been', but that does not mean they will not have a comeback or cannot continue to make a valuable contribution to your events.

CASE STUDY

Stevie Wonder and the RNIB

As probably the world's most popular blind celebrity, Stevie Wonder was an obvious choice to help promote the work and the fundraising activities of the Royal National Institute for the Blind (RNIB). The association between the American pop superstar and the charity began in the early 1980s when Stevie Wonder agreed to footage from one of his videos being used in an RNIB television commercial.

Wonder's first support for an RNIB event came in 1993, when he attended a press conference to launch a series of BT phonecards featuring the RNIB, the profits of which would benefit the charity. At that conference, Wonder made an unanticipated but very welcome announcement that he would be playing a series of special concerts in the UK, with all profits going to the RNIB.

This took the charity by surprise, as they had not been told of the announcement beforehand, but they began to liaise with Wonder's management company to make the necessary arrangements. As it turned out, the series of concerts could not be arranged as planned, but in 1995, as part of Stevie Wonder's European tour, two special concerts were held at London's Royal Albert Hall.

With tickets priced at around £30, the concerts made more than £100,000 in profit for the RNIB. The charity also benefited from another press conference before the concerts. At receptions following each of the two shows, key supporters of the RNIB were able to meet Stevie Wonder.

Lessons learned:
- Patron linked appropriately to the organisation's cause.
- A long term relationship generated greater support later on.

CASE STUDY

Diana, Princess of Wales and the British Red Cross

Perhaps the greatest celebrity supporter of the British Red Cross was the late Diana, Princess of Wales. Her contribution to special events began in earnest in 1995, when she agreed to be patron of the British Red Cross 125th birthday campaign. She first attended the launch of a commemorative major donor club, called the 125 Society. The event was held at Lancaster House, an historic building in the centre of London. The princess helped to attract 250 guests for a champagne party to launch the club and to give information about the organisation's 125th birthday.

In May 1995, the princess attended a special birthday concert by Luciano Pavarotti. It was held on 8 May, the birthday of Red Cross founder Henry Dunant, and a special fundraising dinner was held afterwards, at which both Pavarotti and the princess were present. Large companies bought tickets to entertain their clients, and the evening made over £55,000.

Other events followed, but the princess retired from most of her charitable engagements in 1996. It was not until 1997, when the Red Cross launched its anti-personnel landmines campaign, that she supported the British Red Cross again. The princess made a trip to Angola to see landmine victims for herself, and a BBC film crew joined her to make a special documentary. On her return, the princess agreed to attend the premiere of *In Love and War*, Lord Richard Attenborough's film about a love affair between Ernest Hemingway and a Red Cross nurse. This gave an important impetus to the marketing and ticket sales for the premiere, and with a special supper and fundraising auction arranged at the Savoy Hotel in London after the film, tickets were priced at £150 a head.

The premiere attracted some very special guests, including actor Stephen Fry, Angela Rippon, and the star of the film, Chris O'Donnell. The princess and the BBC also allowed a specially edited version of the Angola documentary to be shown, and Lord Attenborough made an impassioned plea for a global ban on landmines. With the auction and a special prize draw later that evening, the entire event raised over £150,000 for the British Red Cross, and it received considerable coverage in the British press.

Lessons learned:
- Involvement in the charity's work resulted in greater commitment from the celebrity.
- Public interest in the celebrity greatly enhanced the success of events.

7

Launching to the public

Public launches of special events can do much to excite interest both in the media and the general public, encouraging more people to attend the event and promoting your work to a far greater audience than you might otherwise achieve. In fact, holding a high profile launch for your event may be essential if you have to sell a large numbers of tickets in order to reach your break-even point. However, launches are time consuming and can go horribly wrong, so they do need considerable planning.

This chapter will cover the following topics:
▶ Planning the launch
▶ Holding a launch event
▶ Other methods of launching

Planning the launch

Any special event will need to be marketed and promoted long before it takes place. If your event is a major extravaganza, and likely to have a target audience of very busy people, you may need to launch it as many as 9–12 months ahead. Otherwise, two to three months should be sufficient to generate substantial interest in an event, without leaving such a long gap that your potential audience forgets all about it.

Before you go any further in planning a launch for your event, consider who it is that you want to communicate with. Will your target audience be members of the public who are likely to attend the event, or will it be potential volunteers and sponsors who can help you to organise it? Is the event targeting a youth audience, elderly people or those with a specific interest or background? In many ways, the nature of the event will answer this question for you, and in some cases you may discover you need to launch the same event to different potential audiences in different ways.

If, for instance, you are organising a fundraising dinner at a local school, you should be informing the parents of current and former pupils, who may help both to organise the event and to put some money into your appeal fund. Alternatively, if it is a fundraising ball for a hospice, then you ought to be approaching local industry and businesses to buy tickets, not forgetting families of current and past patients who should, of course, be targeted very sensitively. You might also want to use the launch of your event to offer preferential terms or priority booking to existing supporters before opening it out to the general public.

As well as ensuring your launch is held well in advance of your event, you should also check for anything that might compete with it for public attention. In particular, you should avoid the week of Comic Relief or Children in Need, any general, local or by-elections, and you should normally steer clear of Sundays and public holidays, as the media usually run a reduced service on these days. (That said, as these days can be very slow for news, the launch of your event might be picked up by more newspapers and broadcasters than it would be on a crowded weekday.) You should also note the dates of any other key charity weeks, such as the Poppy Appeal and Christian Aid Week, which are promoted widely across the UK.

The choice is ultimately up to you, but whatever you decide, you should not have all the promotion for your event riding on the launch. Keep something in reserve, for even if your launch is a huge success, you will need to maintain awareness and interest in the weeks leading up to the event. If you have the resources and want to achieve truly national coverage and interest in your event, you might also need to plan mini-launches at key locations across the UK to support a national launch event in London or another major city.

Holding a launch event

The means of promoting your event are many and varied and will be determined by the audience you have identified. A press conference or public reception is a good way of reaching large numbers of people, either by talking to those present at the launch or encouraging them to pass information on to others afterwards. Getting the message right is essential. At any launch you should have plenty of representatives from your organisation. They can both speak to the assembled guests and network before or after the launch proper to generate more interest and enthusiasm. Every representative must be clear about the message they are expected to convey.

Make sure everyone at the launch is wearing a name badge, including your own staff and volunteers. This will help to encourage interaction between guests and will also allow your people to know who to target. Make sure some simple materials, such as a leaflet or photographs, are available to advertise the event. If possible, have a video of the work that you hope the event will promote or raise funds for.

The launch of the National Children's Home's Children in Danger campaign several years ago attracted celebrities and public alike to London's Guildhall. Two hundred people signed up to support the event, plus an elephant, which signed with its trunk and subsequently got itself, and the launch, into several national newspapers.

During the launch, challenge your audience to support the event in one of several ways. Ask everyone attending your launch event to do at least one of the following:

- make a donation;
- encourage a friend or business associate to attend the event;
- volunteer to help out on the day;
- donate a gift in kind such as flowers or wine;
- read the promotional literature;
- sign up to a mailing list for future events.

Above all, keep the formal presentations short and to the point. Nothing will get your event off to a worse start than a long and boring presentation to a room full of potential attendees. A sample timetable for a launch event is shown in the box overleaf.

Other methods of launching

If you do not have the resources to hold a launch event, then consider other ways of reaching your target audience. You could place posters in local shops and offices or leave simple leaflets in libraries, doctors' waiting rooms and other public areas. If you have the budget, think about advertising, either through an 'advertorial' (described in *Chapter 9*) or purchasing regular advertising space in the local or national media.

For its programme of activities around anti-personnel landmines, the British Red Cross asked several media owners to donate advertising space in their newspapers and magazines. You too could approach your local newspaper and see if it would offer some space for free or at a heavily discounted rate.

Specialist magazines can offer you readers who are deeply interested in the subject. If you are holding a fashion show, you could try to get coverage in women's style magazines, or an event aimed at children could be promoted in comics or the youth sections included in many newspapers. Again, see *Chapter 9* for more information on this topic.

Sample timetable for launch event

9.00 am	Colleagues arrive at venue.
9.15 am	Make contact with manager of venue.
9.30 am	Erect exhibition stand.
	Check caterers are in place.
	Ensure microphones/lights/staging are in place.
	Ensure backdrop/charity exhibitions are in place.
9.45 am	Be present in reception with name badges and colleagues to welcome guests.
10.00 am	Guests arrive.
	Guests are shown into reception room for coffee.
	Name badges are handed out.
	Colleagues from charity circulate.
10.15 am	Media arrive.
	Media are accompanied to their positions.
10.20 am	Celebrity/guest speaker arrives. Ensure they are taken into a quiet, special room and carefully briefed.
10.30 am	Guests are seated in main hall.
10.35 am	Proceedings commence.
10.45 am	Celebrity/guest speaker delivers speech.
11.00 am	Opportunity for questions and comments.
11.15 am	Conclusion with opportunity for one-to-one media interviews and for colleagues to circulate amongst guests. Literature is handed out to all guests as they leave.
11.45 am	Thank-you to everyone who helped, including caterers, staff at venue, technicians, etc.
11.50 am	Briefing with colleagues to agree follow-up procedures as a result of the event.

Launches can sometimes work well as teasers for the full event, whereby you do not give all the details to the public but just enough to pique their interest. This can be particularly useful if your event has yet to be finalised and you want to gauge public interest before you fully commit yourself to a certain activity or entertainment. If the details of what will happen at your event are still a little vague, celebrity involvement can often be enough on its own to guarantee some press attention. Or, if your chosen venue is unusual, then a press conference or reception held there will probably get people to come along without knowing too much else about the event beforehand.

Checklist for launching to the public:

- Plan your launch at least three months in advance.
- Consider your target audience and desired response.
- Avoid crowded or dead times in the media (e.g. Children in Need, major sporting events, public holidays).
- Create a clear message for the launch and ensure everyone knows it.
- Challenge everyone at your launch to support the event.
- If time or money is short, use posters or leaflets in public places.

CASE STUDY

The British Red Cross Simple Truth concert

In March 1991, in the aftermath of the Gulf War, thousands of Kurds were displaced from their homes, and the media and the general public were horrified by their plight. The British Red Cross wrote to ten impresarios to try to interest them in a fundraising effort to help the Kurds.

The novelist Jeffrey Archer took up the challenge. He had already had the idea of staging a global concert and had talked to the concert organiser Harvey Goldsmith and the BBC. Now he needed a respected international aid organisation to look after the fundraising element, and he chose the Red Cross.

That gave the Red Cross the challenge of coordinating a world-wide campaign, with a concert at Wembley as the centrepiece, which would be broadcast in countries around the world. A date had already been set for the concert – 12 May 1991 – by then just three weeks away. Harvey Goldsmith and his team quickly got on with the job of bringing dozens of stars to London, either in person or by satellite. Meanwhile, the BBC agreed to clear their schedules on BBC 2 and Radio 1 for five hours to broadcast the concert live, when it would create the catalyst for a world-wide fundraising campaign. The Simple Truth concert was born.

The public launch for the event was held in London on 25 April 1991, in front of a packed press conference. Harvey Goldsmith had already signed up some very big names for the concert, including Tom Jones and rap star M C Hammer. In addition, the concert had been promised the front cover of the *Radio Times* in the week of the concert. This was enough to attract the media.

The theme of the campaign was Give us a Fiver. It was important that supporting the Simple Truth seemed a fun thing to do, within the reach of most people. The suggested donation was also a way to gain maximum participation from young people. The pre-publicity for the concert caught the imagination of thousands of children. A small boy from South Croydon raised £5 by not talking during *Neighbours* for a week, while a 14 year old in Berkshire sent in £25 from being sponsored not to watch television. All over Britain youngsters were washing cars, holding bring-and-buy sales, selling raffle tickets and taking part in countless activities to raise money for Simple Truth.

By the time the event took place, the public had regularly been made aware of the concert and the cause behind it. Audited costs of the concert amounted to £100,000 – which were more than covered by ticket sales. There was also the opportunity to sell merchandising and the concert programme. But the most significant result was the thousands of donations that were received from the public, with 60,000 new regular donors recruited to the British Red Cross from this single event. Globally, the concert proved a catalyst for individuals and governments to donate a total of £57 million to help the Kurdish refugees.

Lessons learned:

- Key performers and supporters helped to attract early press attention.
- Low level of requested donation ensured widest possible support from the public.

8

Using your audience

Hiring venues and arranging the entertainment can be difficult enough. Getting paying guests to attend your event and further your cause can be even more fraught, yet success here is critical to the overall success of your event. In the words of more than one event organiser, 'Without an audience, you have nothing.'

This chapter will cover the following topics:

▶ Reaching your target audience
▶ Keeping your audience interested
▶ Asking for support

Reaching your target audience

Very few events succeed purely on the basis that the audience 'wanted to support the charity'. People attend events first and foremost to have a good time, so if they think an event is going to be entertaining, they will pay £10, £50 or £100 for the privilege of being there. That a charity is organising or benefiting from the event will only be a secondary consideration. Competition is tough, so when you market your event to the public, remember that you are competing not just with other charity events, but also with local concerts, the theatre, or even a meal at a good local restaurant.

If your event is of general interest, then begin by targeting your existing 'warm' contacts, that is those people that are known to your organisation and have an interest in your work. This category will include your staff, your volunteers and your regular donors or other, non-financial supporters. From this core group, you can then expand to their families, friends and maybe even their business contacts. This should provide you with a fairly large group of people who might be expected to consistently attend your events, and by doing so could help to defray some of the running costs.

But clearly, if your goal is to raise substantial funds for your organisation or promote its work and messages to new audiences, you must go beyond these 'internal' audiences. You will need to attract others through marketing and publicity, but most of all by matching the event with the likely needs and expectations of your target audience.

If your event is a sporting one, then you can perhaps target sports fans. Do your best to make the event attractive to them – hold it at a local football ground or sports arena, and get some local or national sporting celebrities to turn up on the day, either to compete or just to make a personal appearance. Promote the event through the sporting press, particularly specialist magazines which are likely to be read by your target audience.

Alternatively, if your event is in the form of a fashion show, try to get the latest and most talked about styles on display, because then you will be providing your audience with something they want to see and perhaps cannot see anywhere else. People attending special events will expect a unique experience.

It is worth bearing in mind that, outside of your staff, friends and family, there is rarely a guaranteed audience for any charity event. One major charity learnt this to its cost when arranging a series of concerts featuring performers from the Indian Bollywood musicals. Although the concerts were held in areas with large Asian populations, such as Birmingham and Bradford, very few people turned up to the concerts and they failed to make a profit. The charity assumed it would get support from the local Asian communities, but it failed to research these people's views before it organised the events. They simply were not interested in this type of activity.

Keeping your audience interested

It is important to ensure that your event achieves its objective, and whether that objective is to raise funds or raise awareness of a particular issue, you must engage the audience's interest to meet it. At the very least, everyone who attends the event needs to go away with one new message about your organisation.

Make sure you communicate with your audience at every turn. If it will fit within the timetable, then consider making a short presentation about your work, your campaign or the particular project for which you are seeking funds. If a presentation is inappropriate, then use a small part of the venue for an exhibition about your cause, with eye-catching photographs and perhaps props if they are available. You might consider having some volunteers in costume to promote your particular cause or theme.

Alternatively, you could arrange for the content of the event to reflect your cause. When the British Red Cross had a dance extravaganza to raise money for landmine survivors, banners behind the dancers portrayed images of those injured by mines and carried messages of need. If your charity is helping people who suffer from a particular illness or disability, invite some of those you have helped, or their families, to the event and ask them to talk about your work from their own, personal experience. However, do make sure any speakers are properly briefed, given a set length of time in which to speak and, most importantly of all, meet with them well in advance to ensure they can communicate passionately about your cause.

Give every guest a piece of literature that they can keep. Many larger events will include a specially produced programme or brochure. If you are printing these, or your venue or third party organiser is making them available, then ensure they have at least one page with information and illustrations about your charitable work. Always provide a means for people to make a donation, either offering a reply coupon, or giving your address and telephone number in the programme, as this information will normally be read later at home rather than during the event itself.

If your event will not stretch to a brochure or programme, then simply produce a single sheet of A4, with the same information summarising your work and objectives, which can be handed to people on arrival or, preferably, as they depart. Again, if your audience do not read it at the event, the chances are they will take it home and read it then.

Asking for support

If you are unsure about reaching your audience during the event, then consider adding on a special reception, either before or after the event, at which you can network with your existing and potential supporters in a more relaxed environment. If you do hold such a reception, be sure to include a short, three- to five-minute period during which you can communicate the message of the evening and thank your donors for their continued support.

> When an anti-apartheid organisation hosted Nelson Mandela's first UK public appearance in 27 years, it attracted dozens of leading individuals from showbusiness and industry. Yet it raised no money, because no one from the organisation asked hard enough. Do not make the same mistake at your event.

Too many organisations treat guests at their events with kid gloves. Of course you must acknowledge that they have already shown their support for your cause by attending the event, but that support need not end there. Events can provide an ideal opportunity to begin or further a relationship with individuals who are predisposed to supporting your charity financially.

Do also contact people after the event. It is a simple exercise to thank everyone for attending, and at the same time you can reiterate the purpose of the event. Take time to check the list of those people who attended, and see if there are any particular individuals with whom you would like to build a closer relationship. If so, you can use their attendance at the event as a way into a wider conversation. Always look for the potential spin-offs. A number of charities now write personal letters to everyone who attends a large-scale event. Many ask for further support, such as joining a donor club, volunteering on a committee, or attending a future event.

Checklist for using your audience:

- Target existing contacts (staff, volunteers, donors) first.
- Consider any specialist audiences.
- Tell your audience about your cause.
- Give every guest a piece of literature.
- If necessary, add on a pre- or post-event reception.
- Ask your audience directly for further support.
- Send a thank-you letter to everyone who attended.

CASE STUDY

Yuppies with Puppies and the Family Welfare Association

In the early 1980s, charity balls were popular social fixtures with successful and wealthy professionals in cities around the UK. As a national but little-known charity, the Family Welfare Association (FWA) was aware it had to do something different to attract new supporters to its own events and boost fundraising income.

The FWA realised that many people working in banks and other finance houses in the City of London had yet to be targeted as potential charity supporters. In their jobs, these bankers speculated on the Stock Exchange, so FWA decided to offer them a chance to gamble for charity with an evening's racing at Walthamstow Greyhound Stadium.

Based in the East End of London, the stadium was far removed from the plush hotel venues of the West End, but it had good catering facilities and a large hall that could be decorated to look like a top London hotel. It could accommodate 40 tables of 10 people, so the FWA took its own gamble, booked the venue and began to market the event to the City.

The event was titled Yuppies with Puppies, and a special promotional character, called Gerald the Greyhound, was created. The manufacturers of Filofax, a true symbol of the Yuppy, were based near Walthamstow and agreed to lend their support to the event. Tickets were priced at £40 a head, and companies were invited to sponsor either individual greyhounds or complete races on the evening.

City workers responded favourably to the unique opportunity, and 300 of the available seats were sold. East End celebrities also came forward to attend the event, with Stephen Fry and Hugh Laurie agreeing to supply an after-dinner cabaret. With the help of an additional raffle – which also enabled FWA to capture the names and addresses of these new supporters – the event raised more than £7,000, double the original target. The event subsequently became an annual fixture for Walthamstow Stadium and FWA's growing group of City of London supporters.

Lessons learned:
- Event concept linked to the interests of the target audience.
- New supporters attracted to the event became regular donors.

CASE STUDY

Hey, Mr Producer with the RNIB

When the Royal National Institute for the Blind (RNIB) was offered two special concerts in 1998, to mark the 30th anniversary of theatre impresario Sir Cameron Mackintosh's productions, it thought carefully about the implications before saying yes. The shows offered a real opportunity to introduce potential new supporters to RNIB in the run up to the launch of its Capital Appeal in 1999, not least as the profits from the shows would be spent on some of the appeal projects. One of these, the development of a music project for disabled young people, had engaged Sir Cameron's interest and was one reason RNIB was offered the shows.

While the events, to be held at London's Lyceum Theatre, seemed a marvellous opportunity, RNIB had to sell 2,200 seats on each of two nights to maximise the fundraising potential. With many of the seats priced at £250 each, the charity had a challenge. But the RNIB could bring to the event an element that both Sir Cameron and the paying public greatly desired – the presence of Her Majesty the Queen on the opening night.

The RNIB put together a communications plan, which helped the show to gain an excellent profile in the media in the weeks leading up to the event. As famous performers continued to confirm their appearance, additional press releases were sent out, which helped to sell tickets to those interested in these particular stars. Additionally, RNIB marketed the concerts through individual approaches to its own major donors and key supporters, who were invited to a pre-show reception and after-show party. However, one of the greatest selling points – the first appearance for 20 years of Julie Andrews on the London stage – was only confirmed at the last minute, when tickets had already sold out.

The after-show party attracted many members of the audience – some of them existing RNIB supporters and others new contacts, many of them from companies. RNIB staff were able to mix and delicately talk about future fundraising opportunities. The party also provided extra coverage for the show and for RNIB in the society pages of national newspapers.

Lessons learned:
- Presence of the Queen gave the event a strong selling point to the public.
- After-show party enabled the charity to build relationships with members of the audience.

9

Talking to the media

The media has a history of supporting fundraising events and other activities, from Live Aid, Comic Relief and Children in Need, to the ITV Telethons and Capital Radio's Help a London Child. But far from restricting themselves to their own events, television and radio broadcasters, along with newspaper and magazine publishers, are usually only too happy to support other charitable events and provide invaluable publicity before and after the big day.

This chapter will cover the following topics:
▶ Resourcing your public relations
▶ Approaching the media
▶ Other routes to the media
▶ Paid advertising

Resourcing your public relations

Good public relations (PR) takes time and energy so if at all possible get someone working exclusively on this aspect of your event. Do not expect your event committee chairperson, or even yourself, to be able to handle the press alone. Many charities will have a member of staff or a regular volunteer who looks after all dealings with the media. If you do not, then consider hiring someone for the few months leading up to the event, or alternatively invite a representative from the local media onto your event committee. You might consider the editor-in-chief of your local newspaper, the managing director of your local radio station, or perhaps the regional news presenter on your local terrestrial or cable television station.

If you have a major sponsor for your event, then ask whether they have their own professional public relations staff or whether they have a contract with a PR agency. Do not be afraid to ask a sponsor to help out with promotion for the event – after all, it will have the effect of creating greater awareness of the sponsor's name and involvement as well as your own. At the very least, a sponsor's own PR staff could give you advice and support in writing a news release, or help in identifying who it is best to talk to among the local media.

Approaching the media

Editorial coverage is usually free of charge, but you will need to plan well in advance for this. Monthly magazines often write most articles two or three months before publication, and while newspapers and weekly titles are written much nearer to publication, it does not hurt to give journalists plenty of warning about your event. Publicity schedules will vary depending on your particular circumstances, but a sample PR schedule is shown below.

Media relations timetable for British Red Cross DancePower event	
Late 1998	Advance information sent to dance magazines, BBC, PR diaries
23 February 1999	Information posted on British Red Cross website
1 March 1999	First press release announcing event and photo call sent to national newspapers, listings magazines, Press Association, photo agencies, radio and television stations
8 March 1999	Photo call at event venue
During March	Information on event performers sent to specialist magazines
March/April	Interviews with performers placed in national newspapers and magazines
Early April	Advertisements booked in London newspapers and listings magazines
9 May 1999	Event takes place

The most common form of contact with the press is in the form of a news or press release. As most publications receive dozens of press releases each day, it is important to make your release short and to the point, yet ensuring it still contains the essential facts a journalist will need to know. While an interested journalist might follow up a press release with a call for more information, they should not have to ask you the date of the event, for example.

Your press release should include the type of event you are holding, the venue, the date and time, ticket prices (if applicable), and a contact number for further information. Make sure you give a telephone number that can handle lots of calls if your promotion takes off, as there is nothing worse than people who are interested in attending your event being unable to get hold of you or one of your colleagues. Try to also include a quote from your most senior employee, your event chairman, or your supporting celebrity if you have one. A standard news release for Macmillan Cancer Relief's World's Biggest Coffee Morning is shown below.

Macmillan Cancer Relief pro-forma news release for the World's Biggest Coffee Morning

GIVE MACMILLAN CANCER RELIEF A COFFEE BREAK

.... (name of host) is inviting local people to take part in the **World's Biggest Coffee Morning with Nescafé**, which is being held nationally on **Friday 2nd October**, to raise money for Macmillan Cancer Relief.

The coffee morning will take place at (venue) ....

from (time) .... to .... and money raised will go towards helping local people with cancer.

People living in the area are encouraged to help organisers make the World's Biggest Coffee Morning with Nescafé a fun occasion.

Local host, ... said: "Please do join us for a coffee, the morning really should be fun and it's all for a good cause. The event, which is in its eighth year, won itself a place in the Guinness Book of Records when over half a million people took part in some 15,000 coffee mornings held simultaneously around the country, raising over £1.5 million in just four hours. Macmillan believes it is possibly the biggest participation event in Britain. Absolutely anyone can join in, including schools, local companies and factories. It's so easy!"

For more information, please call (name of host)

.... on (telephone number) ....

ENDS

For press information, please contact (press contact)

.... at Macmillan Cancer Relief on

(telephone number) ....

Start by sending or faxing the release to the diary sections of your chosen magazines or newspapers. Many publications have such a section, which features forthcoming events and gives details for further information. Diary editors will themselves sometimes forward details of more interesting events to their news editors, but there is nothing to stop you directly approaching the news desk of a magazine or newspaper if you feel the event is unusual enough. News desks will often be interested in covering the event if it is to be held at a unique venue, or if a well-known celebrity is due to attend or has offered their support to the event.

Contact details for magazines and newspapers are easily found. Those local to your office or the venue of your event should all be on sale at local newsagents. For more extensive press contacts, you should consult one of several available media directories, such as *PR Newswire* or *PIMS* (see *Resources*). However, these directories cost several hundred pounds each, so it is worth asking a local company or another charity in your area if they have a slightly older copy that you could use as most details change infrequently.

You may find that the media would like to interview someone from your organisation or come and film one of your projects for later broadcast. Think in advance about who would be comfortable being interviewed and which flagship project you would like to promote to the public – perhaps your event is raising money for a specific piece of work, which you could demonstrate to a journalist or television crew.

If you do not want to wait for follow up calls that may never come, one option is to hire a freelance journalist to conduct an interview with your key spokesperson or to make a short video. This interview or video can then be sent to a number of different publications, a process known as syndication. Clearly, this is most appropriate if your event is of national interest and likely to attract an audience from across the UK. Always notify editors if you have approached other programmes or publications with the same material, as this may influence their decision on whether to run your piece.

While most of your press activity will be focused on the lead up to the event, do not ignore potential press coverage after the event has taken place. To achieve post-event publicity, you could send another press release to news editors after the event, or better still, invite journalists or editors to attend the event itself. If your event is ticketed, then reserve some free tickets to send to your media contacts, and if the event is seated, then you might consider creating a special media section if you expect more than a couple of journalists to attend.

Other routes to the media

Many television and radio channels have special community action programmes that can give publicity to your event and perhaps attract volunteers to help you organise them. The BBC, for instance, has a short television programme called *Lifeline* (see *Resources*), which is broadcast once a month and dedicated to charity and non-profit activities. The programme is always looking for stories and is particularly interested in any events that are novel, offer national participation and will promote and encourage support.

Lifeline likes to feature case studies by doing interviews and possibly making challenges. They often encourage viewers to telephone or write in for further information about the event or activity. Any charity contemplating a nationally lead event programme should certainly contact the *Lifeline* producers, who would welcome a conversation to discuss whether the event or activity is something they might feature. Remember, though, that you need to allow plenty of time – speak to the production office at least three months before your event is due to take place.

Radio 4 also features a regular charity broadcast. Indeed, most commercial television and radio stations also run these community action slots, as they are usually a condition in the station's broadcasting licence. Contact the community programmes unit of your local television and radio stations for current details of what they can offer and to find out how far in advance they plan the content for these slots.

You might also consider placing an 'advertorial' in your local or regional newspaper. This is editorial coverage, for example a preview of your event, which the newspaper agrees to publish for free if it can get local businesses to take advertising space around it. These adverts are along the lines of 'John Smith Butchers is pleased to support A N Other Charity's gala ball'. The benefits of an advertorial are that you can have far more control over what is written and published than in normal editorial coverage, and it also enables you to build a relationship with the local companies who agree to take out advertising. Within reason, you should also be able to stipulate the time when the advertorial is published.

Depending on the scale and type of event you are holding, some radio or television stations may be prepared to broadcast your event live or record it for later transmission. Classical concerts are a particular favourite with certain of the specialist radio stations. Broadcasting your event will clearly help to promote your cause and messages to a wider audience; it may also encourage more viewers and listeners to make a donation. However, there are strict rules on issuing appeal numbers during a broadcast (expect for the community action slots mentioned above) so you are not likely to be inundated directly with donations or offers of help.

Paid advertising

There may be occasions when you need to pay money for advertising in the media. Buying advertising space in newspapers or on the radio is not cheap, so you need to plan carefully. One charity some years ago spent £5,000 advertising an event in a regional newspaper. Only a few tickets were sold from the advertisements, with an eventual loss of profit from the event. It is therefore important that you build any likely advertising costs into the original budget from which you will have calculated your break-even point.

That said, there are often good results to be had from paid advertising. A major charity, holding a dance event in London in 1999, spent £9,000 advertising the event in the five weeks before it took place. This resulted in sales of over 750 tickets, which more than covered the costs and brought a new audience to the event. Those people who purchased tickets are now placed firmly on that charity's database, so the advertising bought on that occasion was well worth the expense.

Local radio advertising can also be very effective. Having a celebrity recording a 60-second advertisement, saying something about the event, can get your message to many thousands of people, with hopefully a resulting increase in ticket sales and individuals attending the event. Some radio stations will even help you with the writing and recording of your advertisement as part of the fee that you pay for booking the advertising airtime.

Checklist for talking to the media:

- Appoint a press contact, either paid or unpaid.
- Contact the media well in advance of the event.
- Write a short and succinct press release.
- Speak to BBC or local commercial radio/television stations.
- Ask sponsors to support an 'advertorial'.
- Consider paid advertising in key media.
- Follow up media contacts after the event.

CASE STUDY

BT Voices for Hospices

In 1989 a small fundraising concert was organised in aid of a local hospice in Surrey. While the event was successful at raising money and drawing local attention to the work and needs of the hospice, the organiser Sheila Hurton felt there was an opportunity to extend the event concept and raise funds for hospices across the UK.

The idea of Voices for Hospices was born, but substantial backing was necessary to make it a reality. BT agreed to sponsor the first national event, held in 1991, providing premises for meetings, PR support and management advice, and covering administrative costs. The event that year saw 119 hospices organising simultaneous concerts and sing-alongs around Handel's Messiah, raising £400,000.

BT's continuing support enabled the event to become an annual fixture in the hospice fundraising calendar, both in the UK and in many other countries. The numbers of people taking part steadily increased, as did income from the events. In 1997, BBC Television agreed to promote the BT Voices for Hospices concerts with a special edition of its *Songs of Praise* programme, featuring one of the events in Manchester. BBC Radio 2 also broadcast a concert and further excerpts were carried on the BBC's World Service.

That year, there were 537 concerts in 37 countries, and the BBC's support helped the events to raise over £1 million for the hospice movement. Media coverage was extensive, with more than 1,100 reports in newspapers and coverage on most major broadcast networks. Today, BT Voices for Hospices continues to attract the support of the media and through it a wider public audience.

Lessons learned:
- The event built up steadily over several years to ensure greater success.
- Sponsorship and media support helped to take the event to a wider audience.

10

Running sales and auctions

Charity sales and auctions are an increasingly popular choice as fundraising events. Not only can they be a profitable and exciting conclusion to a longer event, but some are large enough to attract guests and bidders in their own right. However, auctions can also go horribly wrong, with dozens of unsold items and very little income in return for lots of hard work.

This chapter will cover the following topics:
▶ Selecting the best auction items
▶ Inviting an audience prepared to spend money
▶ Briefing the auctioneer
▶ Getting outside help

Selecting the best auction items

The quality of your items for sale, or the 'lots' as they are known in auctioneering, will dictate the potential success of your event. Therefore, when seeking interesting items for sale or auction, consider all possible sources. The most common route is to set up a committee of influential volunteers, who can then use their contacts to find interesting lots for the auction. They will also be able to help locate a suitable and cost-effective venue for the auction and encourage their friends and business contacts to attend.

This committee should be established at least three months before the auction is due to take place. This will allow enough time to find strong auction items that will appeal to potential bidders – if you only leave a month for this, you may still find a dozen lots, but they might not be the most appealing or lucrative. A three month lead-in also allows for a proper marketing campaign to promote your event (see *Chapter 7*).

You will need to decide how many lots you wish to have at auction. If you are organising a large event, then eight to twelve items should be sufficient; if a small dinner, then six to eight items would be more appropriate. Even if your event is solely an auction, do not put up hundreds of lots as the most committed guests will soon get bored, and lots offered late in the proceedings will be unlikely to fetch anywhere near their true value.

Always vary the lots on offer, unless you are running a themed auction such as one of film or sporting memorabilia. Trips to the theatre, holidays, perfume and cars (if you have a generous local dealer) are attractive auction items, and two or three of these, perhaps mixed with other smaller, quirkier lots, would make for an interesting event. Unless you are planning a specialist auction, avoid paintings or other works of art as they are very much a matter of taste and not nearly as likely to find an interested bidder, unless they are by an artist that people are familiar with.

> If you are planning lots of theatre trips or holidays, always try to create a complete package. Two weeks in Kenya are not so attractive to a bidder if they have to arrange their own travel, so bundle flights and accommodation together. Similarly, a night at a West End show will be more attractive to a non-London audience if transport and overnight accommodation are also provided.

Many people and companies who would not normally give large sums of money to charity are happy to donate items, either new or second-hand, that are of no real use to themselves but which could raise a lot of money in the right circumstances. For instance, a major company that is renovating its offices may have works of art which do not fit with its new decorating scheme, but which may be profitably offered at auction. Manufacturing and retailing companies may also be able to donate new products, such as books, electrical equipment, perfume or clothing.

Do not forget to approach your existing supporters for items before committing yourself to the additional time and expense of making a public appeal for auction lots. Celebrities, too, can be a useful source of memorabilia and other items with curiosity value due to their famous owners. A football signed by the striker of your nearest Premier League club could increase the value of that football by 1,000% or more. Opposite is a list of typical auction items, which you can scale up or down according to your likely audience.

> **Suggested auction items**
> - Plane tickets and hotels
> - 2 tickets for a West End show (*Chicago, Cats, Les Misérables,* etc)
> - 2 tickets for a sporting event (Wimbledon, Grand National, FA cup final, Open Golf championship, cricket test match, etc.)
> - 2 tickets for a special event (Edinburgh Tattoo, etc.)
> - A personal item from a celebrity
> - Jewellery
> - Jeroboam of champagne signed by someone famous
> - Wacky idea – e.g. a day at a fire station
> - A new car

Do not underestimate the time and effort involved in assembling a dozen good auction lots. Of course, you may find that your appeal works very well and you receive many more items than originally planned. If you do not think a donated item is strong enough as an auction lot, or you have too many strong items already, check whether the donor is happy for you to keep the item for something else, or whether they expect to see it sold for funds immediately. Remember to resist the temptation to have too many lots at a single auction.

If you do not believe an item would be popular enough at auction, do say so. There is nothing worse than being left with dozens of unsold lots at the end of an event, and lack of interest in weaker items can slow the momentum of bidding on more popular lots. If possible, find an alternative use for the donated item, perhaps as a raffle prize either at this event or another in the future, or alternatively, recommend to the donor another organisation that might benefit from it.

Inviting an audience prepared to spend money

Having made great efforts to secure interesting and potentially lucrative auction lots, it is vital that you attract the right type of people to the auction. Once your lots have all been confirmed, print the details onto A4 sheets of card and distribute these among your committee members. They can promote the lots to their own contacts and perhaps help think of other potential guests whom might be interested in the lots on offer. Those attending must have enough disposable income to allow them to bid vigorously for lots and to reach or exceed the reserve price. They should also have a real interest in the lots on offer.

If you are planning an auction of works of art, invite art dealers, private collectors, and others who have demonstrated affection for the visual arts. If, on the other hand, you are offering sporting memorabilia, you may do better targeting sports clubs and season ticket holders for the particular sports concerned. However, do not target people who are likely to already have the items on auction. When the British Red Cross recently held an auction of holidays aimed at those working in the travel industry, the bidding was fair but it might have been higher with an audience that did not already receive the perk of free overseas trips.

Having identified your likely audience, and invited them to the auction, you should ensure that the event is organised in such a way as to maximise the amounts that your audience will bid. Consider the timing of the auction. Lunchtime auctions, for instance after a meal, do not seem to do as well as evening events, although pinpointing reasons for this is difficult.

Certainly, at a weekday lunchtime auction, guests may be coming from work and may be unaccompanied. This can stifle the larger bids, as people are reluctant to commit substantial sums to an auction lot without consulting their partners. At one lunchtime auction, while a rugby ball signed by the England team was sold for £1,100, a short holiday for two in Dublin with flights and expenses only received a bid of £150. Suppressed bidding certainly seemed to be in evidence here.

In the evening, however, with a suitable ambience and partners by their side, bidders tend to be more active and generous with their offers. However, the timing here is still important, so you should schedule your auction at the most profitable point of the evening. This tends to be immediately after dinner or an evening buffet, as once they have eaten some guests may soon depart for home. Never hold an evening auction later than 11.00 pm. Not only will many people have already left, but those remaining are likely to be too tired to bid enthusiastically or sensibly for your lots, however exclusive and attractive they may be.

The other important element you should consider is the order in which the lots will be placed at the auction. Always save your most valuable item until last, as it will take some time for the auction to build momentum. If your event is solely an auction with, say, three dozen lots then place a high value item every six to eight lots, as this will help to maintain the audience's interest for the full duration of the event.

Briefing the auctioneer

The best selling novelist, Jeffrey Archer, is one of the most successful charity auctioneers in Britain, if not the world. Here he shares some secrets and tips for how the auctioneer should handle things on the night:

The first thing to remember is that at any auction, only about 10% of those people present will be seriously interested in bidding. So make sure that you have enough serious bidders, 20 is ideal, 10 is the absolute minimum, so you will want at least 100 people in your audience.

Having those people sitting in the room is not enough – you must take the auction to them, quite literally. No one will bid a large amount of money for an item they can't see, so make sure there are enough volunteers to act as porters, taking the more portable lots to the tables. After a while you will be able to spot the most serious bidders, and both the auctioneer and the porters should focus on those people. Of course, the auctioneer needs to have eye contact with everyone in the room, so you need to be on a stage or a platform, not simply standing at one of the tables.

If you are working a very large room, it can be difficult to get the right atmosphere and keep the guests focused. If the room is too big for porters to move around quickly, then consider having a large video monitor that can be used to show the lots, and make sure the catalogue includes pictures of all the 'visual' items.

Auctioneers should not bid themselves. I've only done it twice when an auction has been very slow and I've seen a valuable lot going for a pittance; then I've put in a bid to secure that lot so it can be used another time. The dream, of course, is to have two strong bidders competing against each other for an item, and that can happen, but not on every lot.

By far the best way to learn is to visit auctions and observe the style of other auctioneers – the successful ones anyway. You'll soon pick up the techniques that work for them and which you can apply at your own event.

But above all, remember to have fun. Auctions can seem quite nerve-wracking to the beginner, but once you get into the swing of the bidding, and the adrenaline starts to flow, you'll begin to enjoy it, and you'll soon be looking forward to your next event.

Getting outside help

There are lots of hidden costs at auctions, and any charity should be aware of these. You may have to collect donated items from around the country or even from abroad, and arrange for packing and transportation. You will need to pay for valuation and for insurance on the items. Catalogues of the lots are also essential and can be costly, particularly if you have items that need clear colour photographs to convey their appeal.

For help in organising and paying for these ancillary elements, and for general support and advice on your auction, it may be worth considering a partnership with an auction house, particularly if you are planning a large auction with many lots. A professional auction house, like Phillips, Sotheby's or Christie's may agree to host the auction, although they will also normally charge a commission on sales of between 12 and 15%. They may even allow you to promote your auction to their own contacts through a piggy-back mailing, but auction houses jealously guard their mailing lists and are unlikely to allow you to mail their contacts directly.

Checklist for sales and auctions:

- Form a committee to obtain auction items.
- Limit the number of items to be auctioned.
- Ensure a mix of items to attract a wide audience.
- Ask companies to donate unwanted or surplus goods.
- Target people with disposable income and a genuine interest in your lots.
- Hold your auction in the evening and invite couples rather than individuals.
- Brief your auctioneer well.
- Ask professional auction houses for help and advice.

CASE STUDY

The British Red Cross Art Auction

As part of its 125th birthday celebrations, the British Red Cross decided to hold a special fundraising auction of corporate art. Many companies at that time were buying art, partly as an investment but mainly as decoration for lobbies, meeting rooms and canteens. Major corporations were approached to donate some of these paintings and sculptures to be auctioned at a special event in August 1995.

The auctioneers Christie's, who have a long history of charity auctions in support of the Red Cross, agreed to host the event and to help with the approach to potential corporate donors. However, with only three active members on a very small committee, the original plan to get 50 works of art was extremely ambitious. Letters, signed by the chairman of a major bank, were sent to 25 carefully targeted donors, but two months later only three lots had been donated, a figure which rose to just seven lots by January 1995.

Personnel changes at both Christie's and the British Red Cross meant that extra pressure was placed on the small volunteer committee. The British Red Cross appointed a dedicated project manager, which increased awareness of the appeal among companies, but by May, just three months before the auction was to take place, only 13 works of art had been received. The decision was taken to delay the auction until the following February.

With the event delayed, a full committee was formed, with Jeffrey Archer as chairman. Well known artists also agreed to promote the event, and a special reception was held at Christie's to increase awareness of the auction and target corporate donors again. A specially commissioned portrait of the late Diana, Princess of Wales, was unveiled at that reception, which helped to boost media and public interest in the art auction.

With donations and other pledges of support now flooding in, the committee was under increasing pressure to find the lots. By November 1995, over a year since work had begun, still only 35 lots had been acquired, so the auction was delayed again until September 1996.

Corporate leads were almost exhausted by this time, so members of the Royal Academy of Arts were approached, and by March 1996 a further 30 works of art had been donated. A mailing to national newspapers also resulted in 23 signed and original cartoons being offered to the auction.

By May 1996, 103 items were available for auction – a mixture of paintings, cartoons, a few distinguished prints, and a cricket bat signed by the South African cricket team! Invitations to the event were sent to almost 1,000 people, one-third of whom agreed to come on the night.

Christie's held preview evenings for three days before the auction and printed a lavish catalogue to increase interest in the lots. As a result, on the evening of the auction, all but nine lots were sold, raising just over £50,000. With additional donations from those who could not provide auction lots or attend the event, and sales of the catalogue, the final figure raised rose to £100,000.

Lessons learned:
- A committee chairman helped to galvanise other members to obtain auction items.
- Postponement of the event was necessary to prevent failure and potential loss.

11

Celebrating anniversaries

A typical anniversary is a birthday. Everybody has birthdays and likes to celebrate them, so why should charities be any different? Of course they are not, and the significant anniversary has become a popular and important hook for many successful fundraising and campaigning events.

This chapter will cover the following topics:
▶ Types of anniversary
▶ Planning the anniversary

Types of anniversary

Suitable anniversaries can range from a charity's fifth year of operation, the birthday of a famous founder, 100 years since the death of that same founder, a centenary, or any sensible milestone age, such as 25th birthday, 50th or 75th. If you sit down and consider your own charity's history, a potential anniversary to celebrate should not be too difficult to find in the coming years.

If you have no imminent anniversary, you could consider linking to other organisations or companies that have their own anniversaries to mark. The famous London store Harrods, which celebrated its 150th birthday in 1999, opened its doors to many charities, enabling them to hold fundraising events on the premises. Nescafé, also in 1999, involved four different charities in celebrations of the company's 60th anniversary. In 1995, the British Red Cross joined forces with the National Union of Teachers to celebrate the 125th anniversaries of both organisations. There are hundreds of examples of linkages between organisations for the benefit of celebrating an anniversary.

Do plenty of research among any corporate contacts you already have, or those companies based close to your own offices or premises – you might find a department store that is 50 years old, or maybe a factory that has been operational for 25 years. They could share their celebration with your charity and support your cause through their own anniversary activities or events. As mentioned in *Chapter 5*, these piggy-back activities can be a great boon to your fundraising and awareness raising, but do check carefully what you are expected to provide in return.

Planning the anniversary

It is perhaps one of the most important decisions to make before celebrating any anniversary – for how long will your celebrations last? If your charity is to be 10 years old on 4 June, you could decide to have a single event or activity on the birthday itself, a series of events during the whole month of June, or special events at various times during the year. If you are to celebrate over a whole year, make sure you have plenty of activities and events that will maintain the momentum and the interest of both existing and potential supporters.

Once you have decided on their duration, you must ensure that the events you plan have an appropriate style or tone. For instance, if you intend to mark the 100th anniversary since the death of your founder, or a famous local figure who supported your cause, make sure you treat that date with respect. Perhaps you might hold a public ceremony, such as the laying of a wreath, to which the press could be invited, and then follow that with a more lively and celebratory fundraising dinner in the evening to which your supporters could come. If you are celebrating a birthday, then do so in style, making as much noise as possible and ensuring that everybody has fun.

To make the most of your anniversary, and set the appropriate tone for your events, you should do plenty of research into stories and achievements from your charity's past. Talk to people who used to work for you, support you, or those who may have benefited from your services in the past. Not only will you get ideas as to how best to celebrate the date, but some of those people you contact could also speak to the media, or make a presentation at your event, to help publicise the anniversary.

You might also find out which famous people share your birthday. Famous birthdays and special anniversary dates are published each day in *The Times* newspaper and can also be found on its Internet site. You could ask those individuals who share your day to support your event, either by attending as a guest of honour or by donating personal items for auction at the event.

Do ensure that you give the message of your event special consideration. Anniversaries can lead people to concentrate on the past achievements of your charity, forgetting about the vital work it is doing today or what it may contribute in the future. Make sure you develop a clear vision for your cause which can be communicated through the event, and share it with everyone you can think of. Show how the achievements of the past have given rise to your strengths today and the opportunities that face you tomorrow. Think of a slogan, or a strapline for your normal logo, which can help to stress the meaning behind your anniversary celebrations.

Talk especially to your staff and volunteers as the celebration of an anniversary should be promoted internally within your charity as well as externally among the general public. Make sure your own people can contribute to the discussion of ideas and the planning of the events, and invite plenty of them along to the activities as guests as well. This is not only good for internal morale, but it will also make available more people, intimately involved in your work, who can talk to other guests and the local media if they are invited.

Checklist for using anniversaries:

- Link your anniversary to that of other organisations.
- Consider the length of your celebrations.
- Create enough events to maintain momentum and public interest.
- Research stories and individuals from your organisation's past.
- Contact celebrities who share your birthday.
- Involve staff and volunteers in the planning.

CASE STUDY

The British Red Cross 125th birthday campaign

In 1995 the British Red Cross celebrated its 125th birthday. For 18 months it conducted a major fundraising and publicity campaign, unmatched in the organisation's history.

The birthday campaign involved many aspects of fundraising and PR, from sales promotions and special donor clubs, to advertising, commemorative books and other merchandise. But to sustain the campaign for the duration of the 125th year, and beyond, a series of events was planned to keep the momentum going and encourage the widest possible audience to support the British Red Cross.

In January 1995 simultaneous events at 87 football grounds were used to launch the birthday to the British public, a natural link as British Red Cross volunteers provide first aid support at many of these grounds. Clubs around the UK took part, and local celebrities were invited to help attract the interest of the media. In London, actress Jane Horrocks and one of ITV's Gladiators joined Arsenal goalkeeper David Seaman at Highbury for the launch.

From that national launch, the campaign then built to three peaks during the year, each occurring on a significant date. The first of these was 8 May, World Red Cross Day and the birthday of Henry Dunant, founder of the Red Cross movement. The date also falls during Red Cross week, the main period each year for public and street collections by British Red Cross volunteers.

In 1995, this date also coincided with a weekend of VE celebrations, marking the 50th anniversary of the end of the Second World War in Europe. More than 200,000 visitors came to London's Hyde Park during the weekend for official state commemorations, and the British Red Cross organised its own attractions.

On Monday 8 May, the charity held a street party in London's Oxford Street. The street was closed to traffic for five hours, and some 1,250 disadvantaged children were entertained with the support of stores up and down Oxford Street. Over £20,000 was raised through sponsorship from the Oxford Street stores. The street party was opened by the then king and queen of Jordan.

That evening, Luciano Pavarotti agreed to perform at the Royal Albert Hall for a special concert which went on to raise over £55,000. The Princess of Wales attended this concert, and afterwards there was a dinner with the princess and Pavarotti. Prominent businessmen and women bought tickets and the evening was later broadcast by BBC television.

On Wednesday evening of that same week in May, a commemorative banquet was held at the Guildhall in London, attended by the patron of the British Red Cross, Her Majesty the Queen. Marmaduke Hussey, then chairman of the BBC, who had been personally helped by the Red Cross during the Second World War, chaired the event committee. Committee members played a vital role in researching and approaching event sponsors and in targeting potential guests who would be prepared to pay the £125 entry fee on the night. In all, £100,000 was raised from this single event.

The second significant date in the birthday campaign was 4 August, the birthday of the British Red Cross. This was the day that the British Red Cross held its first public meeting in 1870, following publication of a letter in *The Times* from Colonel Robert Loyd Lindsay, who asked the British public to support an appeal to set up a Red Cross Society in Great Britain.

The British Red Cross marked the evening of 4 August 1995 by re-enacting the journey of Colonel Loyd Lindsay, who travelled behind enemy lines on both sides of the Franco-Prussian war to deliver aid to the sick and wounded. Red Cross staff, dressed in the period costumes of 1870, rode through the streets of London to Westminster Abbey, where a fundraising classical concert was held and broadcast live on Classic FM radio.

This was followed by dinner and the lighting of the first of 125 beacons across the United Kingdom. The beacons were chosen to symbolise the fact that the Red Cross 'lights the darkness' for those in need. Supermarket chain Somerfield Stores, which at the time was rebranding itself after years of trading as Gateway, agreed to be principal sponsor for events held at the beacon sites. It approached its own food suppliers for additional sponsorship and gifts in kind. This day generated £1.5 million from the local events.

The third significant date in the year was 23 October, the birthday of the International Red Cross movement. This was the date that the International Committee of the Red Cross held its first public meeting in Geneva in 1861, and so the event on this date in 1995 had a suitably international theme. A special committee, under the chairmanship of volunteer Jonathan Stone, organised an ambassadors' gala. On the night of 23 October dinner parties were held at 15 embassies across London – with the costs of the dinner parties donated by the ambassadors – then later in the evening guests moved to London's Goldsmith's Hall for a gala ball. The event raised over £225,000.

In all, the 125th birthday appeal raised more than £6 million, more than one-third of which came through special fundraising events. This money was in addition to regular fundraising income. The British Red Cross had never before attained this figure with a non-international emergency appeal.

Lessons learned:
- Birthday linked to anniversaries of other organisations.
- Multiple events maintained momentum and appealed to wide range of people.

Conclusion
Lessons for the future

The preceding chapters should have given you some idea of the planning and effort that goes into the most successful special events. At the same time, we hope they have also conveyed the great pleasure that can come from these events and the considerable benefits they can afford your organisation.

Determining your precise objectives, and the nature of your special event, is entirely up to you and your colleagues, but as a final summary, here are 10 key lessons to remember – and apply – when organising any special event in the future.

1. **Set objectives**
    This may seem obvious, but is often overlooked. You should have a clear strategy for your fundraising or campaigning, and any event must fit neatly within that strategy. The objectives should be clear, precise and ideally measurable, so that you can later determine how successful you have been.

2. **Research your audience**
    From your strategy, work out who you need to target to achieve your objectives. Draw up lists of individuals, companies and media organisations who might either support or attend your event, and find out all you can about them. Knowing your audience in advance will save you a lot of money and help to protect you from problems later on.

3. **Agree your budget**
    You must know what your break-even point will be for the event. Carefully work out all possible elements of expenditure and income, and if necessary prepare two or three budgets to take account of variables such as the number of people attending. If you are planning a long time in advance, with some cost elements added in later, then the budget might need to be a rolling one, reviewed and revised periodically in the lead up to the event.

4. **Set your timetable**

   Consider every single activity you will need to undertake, from hiring the venue to selecting the entertainment, from approaching the media to printing the tickets. Be absolutely clear as to when each activity must take place. Consult the timetable constantly to ensure all aspects of the event are on schedule.

5. **Form an event committee**

   From your earlier research into audiences, you should be able to identify likely committee members. Choose individuals whom you can work with and depend upon. Pay particular attention to the chairperson of your committee, as they will need to work closely with you. They must also have the authority to tell other committee members what to do and to remind them if they have not done it. Make sure the committee meets on a regular basis.

6. **Create a control group**

   It is very important to have a systematic approach for monitoring and controlling your plan and budget for the event. Ideally, this should involve a colleague from the finance department as well as the person in charge of organising the event. Such a control group will ensure the timetable is adhered to, that any commitments made are fulfilled, and that the financial targets remain achievable.

7. **Promote your event thoroughly**

   Your timetable should include any marketing, the production of publicity materials and the liaison with the media that is so essential to successful special events. Make sure that everybody working on the event is aware of your key messages and can convey those messages to anyone that they meet.

8. **Evaluate your event's success**

   Not just before it takes place, but during and afterwards as well. Consult your colleagues and even some of your guests, by letter or by telephone, to get objective views of what went well and what went badly. You should also determine whether your original objectives were achieved.

9. **Look to the future**

   Thank everybody that helped out with the event, from your committee chairperson to the owner of the venue, and try to ensure that everyone who was involved would be prepared to support your next special event. If you can look back three or four years after your first event and see individuals from that one still helping out, then you are doing very well indeed.

10. **Keep your enthusiasm**

It is your own energy, and belief in the event, that will carry many other people along with you in the weeks and months ahead. So, remember your cause – why you are running the event in the first place – be calm in the face of problems, and smile!

We hope that these lessons, and this whole book, will help you to bring increased success from your future special events. If you have a success, or even a failure from which lessons can be learnt, then please do share them with us, c/o the British Red Cross. Who knows, in a future edition of this book, your own special event could be teaching your peers and colleagues a thing or two.

Happy special event organising.

John F Gray

Stephen Elsden

Further reading

The following titles are available from the Directory of Social Change, 24 Stephenson Way, London NW1 2DP. Call 020 7209 5151 for a free publications list. Prices were correct at the time of going to press, but may be subject to change. All titles are published by DSC unless otherwise stated.

Fundraising handbooks

Complete Fundraising Handbook
Sam Clarke & Michael Norton, 1997. Price £14.95. ISBN 1 900360 09 8

Finding Company Sponsors for Good Causes
Chris Wells, 2000. Price £9.95. ISBN 1 900360 37 3

Good Ideas for Raising Serious Money – Large-Scale Event Plans
Sarah Passingham, 1995. Price £9.95. ISBN 1 873860 72 2

Law

Charity Law A–Z
John Claricoat & Hilary Philips, Jordans 1998. Price £19.50. ISBN 0 853084 91 2

Voluntary but not Amateur
Duncan Forbes, Ruth Hayes & Jacki Reason, LVSC 1998. Price £14.95.
ISBN 1 872582 22 2

The Voluntary Sector Legal Handbook
Sandy Adirondack & James Sinclair Taylor, 1996. Price £35 for voluntary organisations. ISBN 1 900360 79 X

Finance

A Practical Guide to Accounting for Charities
Kate Sayer, 1996. Price £12.95. ISBN 1 873860 95 1

A Practical Guide to Financial Management for Charities
Kate Sayer, 1998. Price £14.95. ISBN 1 873860 84 6

A Practical Guide to PAYE for Charities
Kate Sayer, 1995. Price £9.95. ISBN 1 873860 33 1

A Practical Guide to VAT for Charities (2nd edition)
Kate Sayer. Available summer 2000. Price £12.95. ISBN 1 900360 62 4

Communication

The Campaigning Handbook (2nd edition)
Mark Lattimer. Available spring 2000. Price £15.95. ISBN 1 900360 63 2

The DIY Guide to Public Relations
Moi Ali, 1999. Price £12.50. ISBN 1 900360 53 5

Management

Essential Volunteer Management
Rick Lynch & Steve McCurley, 1998. Price £14.95. ISBN 1 900360 18 7

The Good Practice Guide for everyone who works with volunteers
NCV, 1998. Price £10.00. ISBN 1 897708 18 1

The Health and Safety Handbook
Al Hinde & Charlie Kavanagh, 1998. Price £12.50. ISBN 1 900360 25 X

Publications not available through DSC

Disability Discrimination Act 1995
ISBN 010 545095 2
Available from the Stationery Office (see *Resources*)

Disability Discrimination Act 1995: Code of Practice
Price £12.95. ISBN 0 11 271055 7
Available from The Publications Centre, The Stationery Office bookshops, or
via the internet: www.disability.gov.uk

Resources

AA Signs
Lambert House
Stockport Road
Cheedale
Cheshire
SK8 2DY
Tel: 0800 731 7003

Airspace Utilisation Section
Directorate of Airspace Policy
Hillingdon House
RAF Uxbridge
Middlesex
UB10 0RZ
Tel: 01895 276108

Disability Discrimination Act
Helpline (for free information about
the Act and the Code of Practice)
Tel: 0345 622 633
Faxback service: 0345 622 611
Textphone: 0345 622 644

Lifeline
BBC White City
201 Wood Lane
London
W12 7TS
Tel: 020 8752 5252 (Main
switchboard: ask for Lifeline)
Website: www.bbc.co.uk

Lotteries Section
The Gaming Board for Great Britain
Berkshire House
168–173 High Holborn
London
WC1V 7AA
Tel: 020 7306 6269

The Patent Office
Concept House
Cardiff Road
Newport
South Wales
NP10 8QQ
Tel: 0645 500 505
Website: www.patent.gov.uk

PIMS
Quadrant House
Regent Street
London
W1R 5PA
Tel: 020 7287 7346

PR Newswire
210 Old Street
London
EC1V 9UN
Tel: 020 7490 8111

The Publications Centre
PO Box 276
London
SW8 5DT
Tel: 0870 600 5522
Fax: 0870 600 5533

RAC Signs Service
1 Forest Road
Feltham
TW13 7BR
Tel: 0845 601 0000

Spotlight Publishing (publishers of
Spotlight)
Tel: 020 7437 7631

The Stationery Office
St Crispin's House
Duke Street
Norwich
Norfolk
NR3 1PD
Tel: 01603 622211
Website: www.tsonline.co.uk